Mysterium Australis

I

Kubrick and the Deep State

Héraclès Harixcalde

Volume I

Mysterium Australis

Kubrick and the Deep State

Understanding Mind Control, Electromagnetic Harassment, and Satanic Wokeism with Kubrick and Jung

1st Edition

En application de l'art. L.137-2.-I. du code de la propriété intellectuelle, toute reproduction et/ou divulgation de parties de l'œuvre dépassant le volume prévu par la loi est expressément interdite.

© Héraclès Harixcalde, 2024
Translated with ChatGPT and verified.

Édition: BoD · Books on Demand GmbH, In de Tarpen 42, 22848 Norderstedt (Allemagne)
Impression : Libri Plureos GmbH, Friedensallee 273, 22763 Hambourg (Allemagne)

ISBN : 978-2-3225-3666-5
Legal deposit : September 2024

"My little finger told me to raise the middle one."
VALD

The richness of the soul is made of symbols. He who possesses the image of the world possesses half of the world, even if what is human in him is poor and has nothing. Hunger, on the other hand, turns the soul into a beast that devours indigestible food and thereby poisons itself. My friends, it is wise to nourish the soul, otherwise, you raise dragons and devils within yourselves.

[...]

You will not overcome the old dogma by doing less but by doing more. Every step that brought me closer to my soul elicited the mocking laughter of my demons, those cowardly poisoners who whispered their sarcasms in my ear. It was easy for them to laugh, for I had strange things to do.

Excerpt from Liber Novus, Liber Primus, The Red Book by C.G. Jung

"He claimed that a machine called the Air Loom kept him under its invisible influence, inflicting agonizing pain and turning his thoughts into gibberish. His elegant technical drawings depicted a machine fuelled by two barrels of 'magnetized gas' and 'putrid effluvia.'

This machine, powered by a windmill, dispensed its mesmeric currents directed at human targets by its diabolical operators. It assaulted the bodies of its victims with tortures, cracking and scraping them with a rasp and a nutcracker and filled their minds with visions of horror."

>Excerpt from « The Influence Machine, James Tilley Matthews and the Air Loom Machine »
>from Mike Jay

"Let us not be men of Galilee; the whole world is our homeland. And our God is not only the God of Jerusalem or Rome.

He is the God of the entire Universe. The synagogue of the Jews believed it alone held promises of Eternity; yet Christ has come once and has abolished the law of Moses by fulfilling it in a more sublime manner.

It is true that Moses foretold another prophet. But did not Christ announce the coming of the Spirit of Understanding, who will teach all truth, and make humanity a family of prophets?"

>Excerpt from « The Bible of Freedom »
>from Abbé Constant

The subject, Stanley Kubrick

A contradictory and brilliant figure, he was perhaps a great spiritual master who, through cinema—a major and comprehensive art form at the intersection of all others—attempted to awaken the Universe in masse to its own decadence and to make it a family of prophets.

It is undeniable that Kubrick's personal and professional experience, close to the elites of this world and immersed in the deep state, pushed him to scatter many secrets throughout his filmography, which is of seemingly infinite depth, secrets that we have not yet managed to see and that I attempt to reveal here.

Truth always triumphs, but it takes time to follow its course. Was Kubrick the messiah we failed to recognize?

NOTE: FOR COPYRIGHT REASONS, ALL IMAGES TAKEN FROM FILMS HAD TO BE REMOVED. TO ACCESS THE IMAGE ANALYSES, PLEASE VISIT THE WEBSITE: HERACLESHARIXCALDE.WIX.COM OR ON TWITTER/X: @HERACLESHARIX or at the following link: https://archive.org/embed/kubrick-and-the-deep-state

Thank you for your understanding.

Table of Contents

Preamble 12

The Australian Ark 16

Chapter 1 – Stanley Kubrick 18
    Early Years
    Philosemite, Antisemite or Realist?
    Kubrick the propagandist
    Kubrick the technician
    Jung and Kubrick
    Vivian Kubrick and Stanley's intention

Chapter 2 – A Clockwork Orange (1971) 27
    Educational System: Non-existent
    Suburbs and Antiquity
    Social Services
    Bars, Drugs, and Electronic Music
    The Successful Author
    The Feminist
    The Police
    The Prison
    Religion
    Psychiatric Treatment
    Karma or machination?
    Serum 114 and Cinematic Bridges
    The Hospital

Chapter 3 – 2001: A Space Odyssey (1968) 49
    Thus Spoke Zarathustra
    The Odyssey or A Brief History of Humankind
    From Unenlightened Apes...
    Family and Telephones
    ...to Learned Apes: The United Nations
    The Pandemic Parallel
    Food
    The Monolith: Transmutation of the Antagonistic Pole
    HAL9000, IBM, AI, and Predictive Analysis
    Art and Humanity
    The Alchemical and Gnostic Vision

Chapter 4 – The Shining (1980) 69
    The Overlook Hotel
    The Job Interview
    Shining and Intuition
    Wendy, Peter Pan and Hook
    Spirits and Spirituous
    Apollo 11
    Monarch Project
    Junk Food and Mind Control
    Radio and the SERCO Hint
    Television
    Cold War
    What does the NASA actually do?
    The Labyrinth
    Jung, The Red Book and the Bloodbath

Chapter 5 – Eyes Wide Shut (1999) 92
    Tom Cruise and Nicole Kidman
    Alchemy, Initiation Rite, Mirrors, and Transformation
    Cinematic Bridges
    The Blue, the Red, and the Rainbow
    Masculine – Feminine / Anima – Animus
    Gentle Doctor
    Adultery / Thought – Feeling
    Parenthood
    Rothschild and Masonic Symbols
    Orgy, Exposure, and Sacrifice
    The Media
    Intermission
    Ziegler and Ziegler's House: A Real Seat of Power
    Watchdogs
    Miller, Millich; Locksmiths and Security
    Sandor: Big Boss, Freudenstein: Key Stone?
    STOP CMB – A Last-Minute Discovery

Chapter 6 – Lolita (1962) 140
    Humbert Humbert and the Golem
    Peter Sellers and Clare Quilty
    The Single Parent Family
    The Ex-husband
    The Swingers
    Dr Zymph

Quilty, the New Mexico ranch, and the Epstein network

Chapter 7 – Dr Strangelove (1964) 111
Atomic Bombs and Zokhov Island
B-52, CRM 114 and Radio-Communications
Communism
Ripper the Samourai, Mandrake and the theory of fluids
Captain Guano: The Dual Industry Key
Paperclip operation and Dr Strangelove

Chapter 8 – Barry Lyndon (1975) 162
NASA Connection
The Death of the Father, the Chief Mother, and Tribalism
Napoleon and Macron
The Seven Years War
Itinerary of an Opportunist: Fraud, Bluff, and Reputation
The Eternal Dissatisfied and Loveless Man

Chapter 9 – Full Metal Jacket (1987) 173
Equality of Opportunity and Collective Punishment
The Vietnam War
The Duality of Man and Legitimate Violence
Speech, Propaganda and Western Mystique

Chapter 10 – Paths of Glory (1957).................................. 188
France, Free masonry et les « Gamelins »
The World War I
Note-Taking, Official Reports, and Abuse of Power
Law, Charisma and Power
The Prison Chaplain
Colonel Dax and Australian Psych. Cunningham Dax
A German Song

Chapter 11 – Deus Ex Machina 200
DARPA, BRAIN INITIATIVE and IBM
Cognitive Warfare, Freedom Fighters and Targeted Individuals
The Air-Loom Machine and James Tilly Matthews: patient zero of cognitive warfare?

Chapter 12 – Heirloom and Opening..................................209
    Heirloom
    Controlling Psychiatric Services
    Nutrition, Fasting, and Self-Sufficient Food Production
    Take Control of Reporting and Data
    Abandon Traditional Media for Direct Information
    Breaking Away from Hierarchical Structures and Reclaiming NGOs
    Applying Legitimate Violence and Collective Punishment
    Decentralization or Butlerian Jihad?
    Ancient Rites and New Cosmology
    Focus on Universal Beauty and Life
    Introduction to Volume 2: Apocalypse according to Héraclès

Bibliography 218

Preamble
Mysterium Australis

The result of a decade spent at the heart of the Australian deep state, this analysis is the cornerstone of the "Mysterium Australis" trilogy, which aims to shed light on Australia's discreet yet significant role in global governance. This first volume, "Kubrick and the Deep State - Understanding Mind Control, Electromagnetic Harassment, and Satanic Wokism with Kubrick and Jung," is a synthesis of the world system based on an in-depth exploration of Kubrick's filmography — cinematic initiatory mandalas of invisible power that I have been dissecting and re-watching for you for 20 years now.

There is a general theme in Kubrick's work that, it seems to me, has not been properly explored: that of Western mysticism, the "forge of events," and mind control. We are talking here about the all-seeing eye at the top of the pyramid. It is highly likely that the lack of in-depth analysis is a consequence of censorship by omission or controlled opposition, because understanding his filmography correctly means questioning the 20th century, as it details the workings of deep power and the globalist establishment, its objectives, methods, hierarchy, and actors.

For this reason, Kubrick had to address the subject in an opaque and hermetic manner, navigating a fine line that allowed him both to produce films without external influences, maintain economic subsistence, and achieve blockbuster audiences. The subjects discussed here would have endangered his life and that of his family if they had been too obvious and explanatory in a simple viewing. Thus, you will undoubtedly be surprised by some conclusions drawn in certain analyses, which are counter-intuitive and against the grain of usual Kubrick analyses.

I produce this analysis for anyone willing to take the risk of reading it because I feel the responsibility and because it is indispensable and urgent to bring it to light in the face of the emergence of artificial intelligence, the struggle for its control, and the means deployed for the establishment of a world government. These events are happening subtly as I write these lines, at the highest levels, in principalities and supranational organizations. The unveiling of this world system is underway, and if I am permitted to write these lines and this document has reached you—not without great suffering on my part in its production—it is because, somewhere, at the highest level, I have been authorized to do so and the time for official recognition has arrived.

A generalized awareness of the world system and its mechanisms now seems to be the only bulwark against the looming technological enslavement, or one that may have already taken place, but which is not absolutely irreversible and which, if we believe *2001: A Space Odyssey*, could prove to be beneficial to humanity provided we possess the technical knowledge and mastery of the control mechanisms, which are above all spiritual.

In this regard, I would align with the analysis of a certain Harari, with whom I do not share the same value system, but who seems to be the only initiate with authority and publicity on the description of the future of humanity and the advent of a sentient AI that now governs and guides all our social interactions. This is facilitated by their profound knowledge of our souls enabled by surveillance, Big Data, and materialized in the form of suggestions or controlled synchronicities, micro-punishments, micro-rewards, and a new form of social engineering.

It is now clear that the 20th century was a struggle for the control of this technology more than any other, driven by science and the military. This technology's ultimate objective is mind control and the subjugation of the population, which resulted in two world wars, two atomic bombs, and very likely a third conflict to come, or one that is already underway.

The question at play in the 21st century is the programming of the value system that determines community life, social relations, good and evil, and the preservation of free will, at the risk of transforming humans into *Prima Materia*, human resources, or even into foodstuffs for an industry without governance and moral authority. It is high time for a return to spirituality, a confrontation with the shadow as described by Jung, enabling men to have communion and a direct relationship with God, and the rejection of toxic hierarchies to break the vicious circle in which we find ourselves. This confrontation can make each person a Christ, a Buddha, or a prophet, upholding a positive ethic through self-reflection and soul-searching, and a rediscovery of the heart and charity in an age of boundless narcissism and materialism.

Kubrick's work, like that of Leonardo da Vinci or the great architects who hid within their works the keys to understanding the recent and ancient universe, the cosmos, and the "coming change," is a compendium of examples not to follow, examples of a derailed society controlled by obscure spiritual forces that have taken possession of the global governance matrix. Provocations today are legion and demonstrate the omnipotence of this network; from drag queens in elementary schools or the Vatican, to the pharmaceutical industry and hospitals that promote euthanasia and deny doctors the right to heal. The once useful and productive world of village priests has derailed in favour of parasitic hierarchies of gilded offices: humanity has sold its soul for a meagre salary to the Woke ideology and its mediocrity, in a spectacle that would make Burgess's A Clockwork Orange blush.

In the following analysis, I will attempt to link each of Kubrick's films to the themes of occult power and mind control, establishing connections with Jung's major spiritual work, while deductively and intuitively identifying the largely unexplored revelations of Kubrick's filmography that will initiate a collective research and historical rewriting.

I hope this study will one day soon serve a return to a stronger ethic and recognition of the abuses and tortures by Western governments who control neurobiological and electromagnetic weapons. Unfortunately, we have been victims of the devil's trickery and made the mistake of believing he did not exist, thus overlooking the importance of self-sacrifice and legitimate violence.

The poem "The Australian Ark" will serve as an introduction and mnemonic device to facilitate access and re-access to Kubrick's filmography and its analysis. I recommend the reader to have recently watched his films or to watch them while reading, as the many sensitive secrets are revealed here through hidden details.

I will start the analysis with a selective biography of Kubrick's life, which will allow us to set the context for the analysis, particularly his family relationships and social and professional context, and to understand his personal intentions. In our analysis, we will omit his minor films, which do not fit into this research (The Killing, Spartacus, Fear and Desire). The analysis is thematic and not chronological, with Eyes Wide Shut in the central position, the cornerstone of his filmography but incomprehensible without the concepts presented in A Clockwork Orange, The Shining, and 2001: A Space Odyssey.

I will strive to maintain simple language and a concise form as much as possible to make it accessible to the greatest number. I will clarify any ambiguities on social media (X/Twitter) if there are any, as I write these lines in haste and you have here the first edition that will be enriched by future discoveries; if it is imperfect, I hope it will be a good starting point for thorough and collective research.

If the analysis sometimes seems obscure and the themes pessimistic, rest assured that all paths here lead to the same conclusion: let us have heart, abandon bureaucracy, and turn to God.

The Australian Ark

Full Metal Jacket
Children? In camps, soldiers they became: a collective fate.
In Vietnam, soldiers and reporters, sharing the same weight:
"To see the foe, just once, a tale to narrate,
Where we're not the villains and enemy is a man"

Paths of Glory
As a Gamelin at his desk commands each mission,
While at the frontline, children tread the glorious path wide.
For a franc they execute, they perish, per million's tide,
Yet they may still shed a tear for a German song.

Orange Clockwork
At truce, on electro beat, youth quenched by Moloko's brew,
In rapes and violence, reptilian headspace they sharpen.
Social services, asylums, prisons their new curriculum,
And from a hospital bed, politics tomorrow they'll pursue.

Barry Lyndon
Grown up, the rancour from incestuous love stain,
Propels him to glory and adventure, seeking to forget the pain.
He plays, he gropes, he cheats, forging his own game,
But the debt beware! It is sickness, without knowledge or reign...

Shining
Writer, mystic of skill devoid, priorities in lunar sway,
In Cold War America, cornered, he plays the barman's way.
"Wife and children?" "Just a little, let me work, I pray."
"For television?" "Perhaps! a place in Pantheon's array!"

Lolita
Fleeing, a smooth talker he now fashions himself a sage.
But Lolita, to the Golem prefers the stage.
To Epstein, ancient producer, in Mexican mansions engage,
Sold her soul to Evil - Sue Lyon seeks paternal page.

Eyes Wide Shut

Mocked by his wife who desires military lover,
Naive doctor gets initiated by Manhattan and Ziegler
Into High Kabbalah, where Israel kings and tribes' hover
In pagan orgies and blood rites: no U-turn there.

2001 Space Odyssey

Monoliths and exponential progress, a minister multi-planetary,
Engages Earthlings, once kin, with new mobiles and fake pandemics,
While HAL, immortal conscious processor, superior AI algorithm,
Multiplied by the Eclipse, devours Languages, Images, and Memory.

Dr Strangelove

Nuclear Apocalypse is shed from madness, suggestions casted
To a mundane Scapegoat, Admiral protecting vital pineal gland,
Saved shall be chosen ones by Semite Doctor or Nazi Noah,
And by magic: bunkers, rations and women: the Australian Ark.

CHAPTER I
Stanley Kubrick

Here, we will attempt to situate Kubrick within his familial, "political" environment, and his significant relationship with Judaism, to better grasp his theses, describe his method and technique of staging, which will allow us to understand the importance of detail in Kubrick's work, and the non-trivial aspects of those details. Nothing in Kubrick's films is left to chance, and it is crucial to understand the author's intentions, which have never been publicly articulated. We will briefly analyse the recurring connection of Kubrick's works to those of Jung, as well as the personality of his favourite daughter, Vivian Kubrick, which will lead us to intuitive reasoning, a mindset necessary for the symbolic and in-depth understanding of his oeuvre.

Early Years

Kubrick was a New York Jew from a well-to-do Romanian-Austro-Hungarian family. His father was a cardiologist, pianist, and photographer who introduced Kubrick to chess. On film sets and throughout his life, Kubrick often played chess with his collaborators, a game referenced in *2001: A Space Odyssey*. His films, much like a chess game, frequently lead the audience in one direction only to take them by surprise.

His mother, a dancer and singer, instilled in him a love for music and literature. Kubrick likely received an excellent education from his parents, providing him with great confidence and a taste for art and perseverance due to their respective professions. He showed little interest in school, finding the courses too boring and standardized for energetic young people, a vision reflected in *A Clockwork Orange*.

The family never formally practiced Judaism, but their library was well-stocked with works by modern Jewish authors like Freud, Kafka, and Zweig, whom Kubrick was encouraged to read. This likely nurtured his Jewish spirit indirectly. Moreover, his grandmother spoke Yiddish, and he had some knowledge of it himself. His first two wives, Toba Metz and Ruth Sobotka, probably also spoke Yiddish as they were from the first generations of Jewish migrants from Europe. Both marriages ended in failure.

Influences and Personal Life

Born in 1928, Kubrick grew up during the rise of Nazi Germany following World War I and reached adulthood at the end of World War II. It is likely that his worldview and political views were heavily influenced by his parents and the stories of his newly emigrated Jewish companions about the conflicts in Europe.

However, it was with Christiane Harlan, the niece of Nazi propaganda filmmaker Veit Harlan, that Kubrick spent his life. She appeared on screen in *Paths of Glory*. His early years in the Bronx likely surrounded him with the resourceful youth of Manhattan, which may have helped him develop the characteristics necessary for survival in the show business world, especially those of a merchant and entrepreneur.

Kubrick began early, in his adolescence, with photography, where he honed his knowledge of the camera and his structuring of images, before embarking on directing short films, with an economic gain in mind.

Philosemite, Antisemite, or Realist?

Kubrick's stance towards Judaism presents a certain ambiguity, especially considering his marriage. Veit Harlan, Christiane Harlan's uncle, was the director of *Jud Süss*, a film that portrays a particular vision—real or illusory depending on one's perspective—of supposed rabbinical methods used to subjugate the Stuttgart court through usury, corruption, and moral perversion. This film is often cited as a prime example of Nazi propaganda. Veit Harlan himself married the German Jewish singer Dora Gerson in his youth, whom he was forced to leave due to pressure from her family over his non-Jewish background. This could explain a certain resentment or animosity Veit might have had towards the Jewish community.

Kubrick was very close to his in-laws, moving closer to them by relocating from the United States to England after purchasing Childwickbury Manor in 1978, which he used as a studio, making his filmmaking a family affair. His daughter and in-laws were involved in the film shoots and editing, and his brother-in-law, Jan Harlan, alternated roles between assistant and producer.

The Jewish-American director Dalton Trumbo, author of the *Spartacus* screenplay, accused Kubrick of being a Jewish antisemite. Trumbo reported Kubrick's words from their conversations: "He told me that Jews were responsible for their own persecutions because they separated themselves from the rest of humanity." Elsewhere, in his memoirs on *Eyes Wide Shut*, Frederic Raphael recounts Kubrick's remark: "Hitler was right about almost everything."

Additionally, as his wife Christiane Harlan confessed, Kubrick never responded to antisemitic attacks or boycotts, which he often faced. He seemed to understand the hostility that his belonging to the Jewish community could generate. His behaviour reflected that of a misunderstood yet tolerant man, who might say something like, "maybe one day you will understand what I meant."

One can't help but wonder what his vision of the Holocaust would have been if he had had the chance to make a film on the subject, as was planned. He spent many years studying and compiling research for such a film, which reportedly made him "nervous and depressed," according to his wife. This preparation was for the film *Aryan Papers*, which was never made, allegedly due to the release of *Schindler's List*, among other reasons.

Kubrick's intricate and often contradictory relationship with his Jewish heritage and the Jewish community is mirrored in his works and life choices. His refusal to clearly align with or against certain perspectives leaves a complex legacy that continues to intrigue and puzzle scholars and fans alike.

In his choice of actors, Kubrick frequently employed actors of Jewish origin, though not exclusively, and he often described himself as "not identifying with any of the monotheisms," despite many of his films referencing divinity (*2001: A Space Odyssey*, *Eyes Wide Shut*). As we will see in the following analysis, Kubrick was primarily a "gnostic," whose quest was for profound Truth, whether found in science, history, psychology, or esotericism. He judged people by their character and competence rather than by their origins, seemingly holding a grudge against tribalism in general, as depicted in *Barry Lyndon* and *2001: A Space Odyssey*, and particularly against the "organized community" of which he had deep knowledge.

Kubrick the Propagandist

Kubrick's genius lies in his ability to be both a master propagandist and a denouncer of the deep state. Early in his career, as seen in *Paths of Glory* (1957) and *Lolita* (1962), he highlighted the practices of the elite, Freemasons, and networks of prostitution and blackmail, which are now widely recognized through the Epstein network. Ambitious and talented, Kubrick made a place for himself within the elite he exposed. He was well-versed in cutting-edge scientific research, interacting with NASA employees, IBM technicians, and always up-to-date with the latest advancements in computing, microprocessors, and other developments in the miniaturization of computers and administrative procedures, as seen in *Dr. Strangelove* (1964).

He likely had connections with the military-industrial complex, as evidenced by his collaboration with Arthur C. Clarke, a science fiction author and former radar specialist for the Royal Air Force. After the release of *2001: A Space Odyssey*, he obtained total artistic freedom and an almost unlimited budget for his subsequent films from his production company, Warner Bros. Or perhaps this was the deal he negotiated to keep the secret around the moon landing and the hoax he was allegedly tasked with, as we will explore in the analysis of *The Shining* (1980).

Among the films he did not make were *Aryan Papers* and *A.I. Artificial Intelligence*, the latter of which he passed on to Spielberg, another prominent Jewish-American propagandist. *Aryan Papers* was set to address World War II, which would have completed his series on global conflicts: the Seven Years' War (*Barry Lyndon*), World War I (*Paths of Glory*), the Cold War (*Dr. Strangelove*), and Vietnam (*Full Metal Jacket*). What did he discover during his research for *Aryan Papers*? We will likely never know.

Was Kubrick tasked by the establishment to hasten the fall of the American empire by highlighting and exacerbating its negative aspects? Was he a counterforce to the military-industrial complex, or was he in their service? What about the media? Did he serve the interests of the deep state, or was he an independent individual imposing a morality born from his own analysis?

His deep inspiration from Jung raises further questions: Was Kubrick part of a secret organization unknown to us, possibly the same one Jung belonged to? Were they "Illuminati," as some speculate? Or were they simply brilliant individuals in their own right?

Many questions remain difficult to answer precisely, but these two "technical artists" have undoubtedly shaped mysticism, the soul, and the collective unconscious in an irreversible way. We may find a starting point for understanding Kubrick's deeper intentions in the analysis of his daughter Vivian.

This exploration reveals the intricate and often contradictory layers of Kubrick's relationship with his heritage, his work, and the powerful forces of his time. His films, rich with symbolism and nuanced storytelling, continue to provoke thought and debate, reflecting a mind that sought truth beyond the surface of societal norms and expectations.

Kubrick the Technician

Kubrick is reputed to be a perfectionist; therefore, none of the elements that appear on the screen or are suggested off-screen are left to chance. Dialogues, character names, and all the objects placed before your eyes are carefully weighed and measured, like hieroglyphs in an Egyptian tomb. The director relies on your intuition, intelligence, and personal experience to decipher them. One must learn to read Kubrick, as his works are meticulously written.

The writing and design of his films take many years, during which he collects all available information, studies the subject, research shooting locations, and refines the storyboard down to the smallest details. He meticulously selects his actors to serve the writing and expression above all, and his choices sometimes serve as subliminal messages.

Kubrick's staging is strict, structured, dynamic, symmetrical, and symbolic, drawing inspiration from the structure of great painters and the best pre-war filmmakers. Photography being his specialty, the lighting is extremely controlled, something modern digital cinema has lost. His direction of actors is rigorous, often requiring actors to redo scenes up to 80 times, necessary to put them in the psychological state conducive to the role, which involves a certain level of torture. The shoots are long, and the sets are custom-built. This adds weight to his message and enhances his aura. The music is orchestrated, the editing is expressive, and the transitions are meaningful, giving the whole a unique and mysterious aspect, sometimes difficult to access due to its density and depth, which could be termed Kubrickian hermeticism.

Kubrick's technical pinnacle is reached in *2001: A Space Odyssey* (1968), and he maintained this standard until his final work, *Eyes Wide Shut* (1999), released after 10 years of absence and preparation. The release of *Eyes Wide Shut* coincided, strangely enough, with the director's death, and we will see why in the following analysis.

Jung and Kubrick

Kubrick constantly references Jung: in *2001: A Space Odyssey*, HAL talks about transference; in *Lolita*, Dr. Zymph speaks about libido repression; in *Full Metal Jacket*, Joker refers to the duality of man; and the entirety of *Eyes Wide Shut* explores the concepts of anima and animus.

Jung, the psychoanalyst, is considered the mystical genius of the 20th century, who brought to the West the concepts of synchronicity, personality typology, and archetypes. He spent his life exploring the depths of individual and collective psyches. Recognized as a gnostic or a "Christian kabbalist," Jung reestablished an Aristotelian understanding of the soul, highlighting the commonalities between different religions and mythologies rather than their differences. His contributions extend to the popularization of Eastern yoga in the West and the understanding of mandalas, trees of life, and alchemical symbols.

To understand Kubrick's cinema, which is as intellectual as it is intuitive and symbolic, it is worthwhile to familiarize oneself with Jung's work, which lies at the intersection of science, alchemy, and mythology. Discovering Jung can be done through his books *Modern Man in Search of a Soul*, *The Archetypes and the Collective Unconscious*, and finally *The Red Book*, his mystical and symbolic work that could potentially replace the Bible, sooner rather than later.

As often as possible in the following analysis, I will draw connections to Jung's work.

Vivian Kubrick and Stanley's Intentions

To understand that Stanley Kubrick lives on in his daughter Vivian, one must watch an interview with the young Vivian Kubrick at Elstree Studios. It's as if Kubrick himself speaks through the 20-year-old woman. Vivian participated in the making of several of his films, including Barry Lyndon and Full Metal Jacket, and from a very young age, he took her under his wing. It also seems that Kubrick did not reveal to her the deep secrets hidden in his films or the knowledge he had about the deep state, to protect her.

Vivian Kubrick has been very active in the "conspiracy" and QAnon spheres. For instance, she has called Bill Gates a "bioterrorist" and opposed all COVID-19 vaccinations. An exploration of Vivian's Twitter posts reveals her fiercely and passionately opposing the deep state, though perhaps in a naiver manner than her father. Indeed, it seems her father knew his enemies well and the risks involved, whereas Vivian's fight ended abruptly in 2021, likely due to pressures she faced, which pushed her, like others, to withdraw from a battle that seemed doomed from the start.

While Vivian denies that her father filmed the Apollo 11 videos in a studio, she justifies it by saying that her father "would never have collaborated with the American deep state," portraying him as a resistor, which again shows her naivety. It's clear that in 1968, the young and ambitious director Kubrick saw the opportunity to mingle with the world's leaders, and The Shining is simply his apology to Vivian and the world for the lie he signed with his own hand, whether she acknowledges it or not.

Notably, at 40, Vivian joined the ranks of Scientology, as did Tom Cruise, something Stanley strongly opposed. One might then wonder to what extent she was influenced by Scientology, especially in her recent stances, and on the choice of Tom Cruise in Eyes Wide Shut. This choice is probably not coincidental, as he is depicted as the useful idiot of a global satanic cult, whose summit has moved from Manhattan to Sydney.

CHAPITRE 2
A Clockwork Orange (1971)

At truce, on electro beat, youth quenched by Moloko's brew,
In rapes and violence, reptilian headspace they sharpen.
Social services, asylums, prisons their new curriculum,
And from a hospital bed, politics tomorrow they'll pursue.

Stanley Kubrick's *A Clockwork Orange* is perhaps his most explicit exploration of deep power structures, surveillance society, and mind control. The film also addresses the state of modern youth. Although the themes here have been extensively discussed, I will introduce new and subtle elements to serve our broader analysis, providing a comprehensive review for readers just discovering Kubrick's vast and surprising filmography.

Based on Anthony Burgess's dystopian novel, *A Clockwork Orange* anticipates the youth culture of the 2000s, steeped in electronic classical music and ultra-violence. It is a psychological novel centred on Alex, a young delinquent caught up by his karma.

The film is a detailed exposition of the layers of civil society and its mechanisms of control, maintenance, and intergenerational power transfer. We will examine how the ruling caste of the state, through a system of selection and profiling, surveillance, and blackmail via various institutions, programs its "Manchurian candidates" with both carrot and stick. In other words, we will explore how the CIA and the deep state, relying on social services and the police (kings on the chessboard), through the MK Ultra project, format pawns, bishops, and rooks to serve the media narrative and maintain their power.

With the official acknowledgment of directed energy weapons through the Havana Syndrome scandal, we now see a myriad of isolated individuals online, labelled by mainstream media as conspiracists or "tin foil hats," identifying themselves as "targeted individuals." These individuals report symptoms they attribute to organized harassment using new technologies and techniques, often involving public authorities and the medical network, without any apparent reason.

Alex's treatment in *A Clockwork Orange* seems to have become widespread, manifesting in a new, more or less invisible, pernicious, and indefensible form of control—a systematic "hazing" of dissenters or what I term "free nuisances."

Educational System: Non-existent

From the system's perspective, it is crucial that youth do not elevate themselves or develop solutions to their problems, and certainly, they must not be able to unite. It is easier to manage two groups of four "droogs" than one group of eight, as one can be used to beat the other.

Alex's parents—his mother with purple hair and his notable yet numb father—are mired in consumer society and their new household appliances, hypnotized by their television set. They appear estranged and fearful of the teenager occupying a room in their house. Alex is easily replaced by a foreign student, providing polite company and rent, highlighting the division, distance, and substitutability of family members today, or the contempt towards a selfish child offered to the deep state's machinery.

Alex skips school, preferring to accumulate easy money and spend his time drinking various "molokos" with his gang. School is never shown on screen because it has become a place of indoctrination into radical left "Woke" ideas, which have seemingly reached their peak in gender identity—the final stage of brainwashing, with the ultimate goal being the lucrative sex change operations, supported and subsidized by the system. Alex has consciously or unconsciously understood this, distinguishing himself from his peers by his aristocratic traits, good looks, and "classic" and virile culture. A fan of Beethoven, opera, fine clothes, and beautiful women, it is suggested that his education came from reading Henry Miller or under a charismatic Greek classicist mentor, from whom he inherited his persona and the complex slang he uses with his droogs to assert their differences.

The only moral lesson Alex receives is from an old alcoholic tramp, representing a future version of himself, whom they torture under a bridge. The tramp laments about society, the lack of respect from the young towards the old, and the government's abandonment of the lower classes. While he is right, he is also accompanied by his empty bottle of wine. In ancient societies, the elders' status as educators was supported by their wisdom and peace of mind.

This tramp symbolizes a failed life and the Sword of Damocles hanging over young men who do not take control of their lives. Beyond a certain age, a man is worth nothing, abandoned to the margins even by community organizations and replaced by young people with equally few values but still possessing their young arms to sell.

In this context, and in a time of peace, the only motivations for our protagonist are money, thrills, and women. The social contract, supposed to be defined in education and school, is broken. The old failures are punished by the young, future failures. The loop is closed in this ouroboros that Kubrick so masterfully depicts.

After this failed human sacrifice, Alex puts away the python symbolizing his reptilian brain and taste for blood, along with his dirty money, locked near his bed.

Suburbs and Antiquity

"Image 1"

In the bland, soulless English suburb where *A Clockwork Orange* unfolds, remnants of antiquity, covered in graffiti and scribbles, can be seen. The columned temples, where once ritualistic and codified drug consumption for divine illumination took place, have been replaced by apartment building lobbies where synthetic products are exchanged for payment to overcome the affliction of boredom. Modern brutalist architecture depresses and resonates with the filthy streets seemingly abandoned by public maintenance services.

In an abandoned theatre, young thugs reenact gladiatorial battles by beating up a rival neo-Nazi gang. These scenes are choreographed like a circus or wrestling match to fill a deep lack of direction and satiate an excess of testosterone, under the paternal gaze of Zeus. The once-sacred ancient theatre, where cathartic and expiatory simulations took place, now hosts real ultra-violence observed by the deep state rather than a public that has moved on to cinemas.

This setting echoes the London nightclub "The Church," where every Sunday, in what is actually an old theatre, great drinking and drinking games for depraved youth take place, a reference to the sacred Sunday Mass. Today, we see a return to the healthy violence of arenas through MMA and its various competitions, new virile, positive, and regulated substitutes for gladiatorial combat, channelling youth who might otherwise spill their energy in negative directions.

Social Services

After a turbulent night with his droogs, our protagonist receives a visit from a social worker. This stressed, perverse little man seems very worried about not meeting his hierarchy's objectives; Alex is a sort of client he must integrate into society one way or another. A prison sentence for Alex would negatively impact this little man's career, and he makes it clear that Alex should behave, painfully squeezing his testicles to emphasize the point.

What's interesting here is the responsiveness of social services. The day after his escapades, a state representative shows up in person. We learn that Alex has had previous run-ins with the law and is on a kind of probation. It also becomes evident that the government deploys significant resources to profile and quickly gather information, shared between social services and the police. There is an immediate sense of a form of monitoring, and their actions, though localized in the closed and derelict space of an old, abandoned theatre, have not gone unnoticed by the deep state.

It is likely that Alex's Droogs are also under surveillance by these same services, which explains the betrayal that follows, turning them into law enforcement officers. Here, we see the sketch of an all-seeing eye and its mechanisms, where the police and social services collaborate. Keeping in mind that in the original book, Alex is only 13 years old, let us draw a modern parallel: due to the destruction of the family structure and the removal of the father's role, education increasingly relies on state services of well-informed but poorly federating small officials. Instead of training young people in combat sports, theatre, or circus, they are inundated with electronic music, exposed to vices while their behaviours—encouraged on one hand— are punished on the other to maintain control.

Upon a worried mother's request, a troublesome man can easily lose custody of his children; the worst-case scenario for the child being placement in foster care. The equation of economic decline and falling education levels quickly overwhelms social services, which, since COVID-19 and the chaotic governance it brought, have transformed into golden platforms for vultures of all kinds.

Now, imagine the following scenario: social services for child welfare, with close ties to the police on one hand, the media on the other, and finally the judiciary. This is what is called full powers, and it is what we are witnessing in the West, in France, and in Australia, subtly depicted by Kubrick here.

Bars, Drugs, and Electronic Music

The gang frequents a gloomy bar, decorated entirely in black with naked female mannequins serving as tables, reminiscent of the orgy in *Eyes Wide Shut*, where mannequins are replaced by flesh-and-blood beings. This is a place for drug-taking before their exploits, thefts, rapes, human sacrifices, etc.

The bar's patrons are other gangs of young men and women with similar appearances but distinct recognition signs, most of them seemingly coming down from various substances. Also present are guards, whom we will call "watchdogs"—a concept we will present in *Eyes Wide Shut*. These bearded men silently observe our companions' actions and report them somewhere.

"Image 1"

The bar frequented by Alex and his droogs also hosts individuals from the upper echelons of society, including showbiz stars and media personalities. These high-profile patrons share a passion for Moloko, notably an opera singer whose rendition of Beethoven's Ninth Symphony triggers an unconscious reaction in Alex. He violently punishes a comrade who fails to respect this rare spectacle, showcasing his tyrannical leadership, which isn't well-received by all.

This setting parallels the real-life scenarios of famous personalities frequenting such places, reminiscent of controversial outings like those of comedian Pierre Palmade. The bar's menu features four drinks: Moloko Plus, Moloko Vellocet, Moloko Synthemesc, and Moloko Drencrom. These correspond to various substances: MDMA (ecstasy), synthetic mescaline (similar to LSD), Percocet (oxycodone or ketamine), and adrenochrome. The latter is notorious in conspiracy theories about Hollywood stars trafficking it for its hallucinogenic, spiritual, ritualistic, rejuvenating, and exclusive properties. This seems to be the drug of choice for Alex.

Aside from adrenochrome, these substances are widely available at raves, techno parades, and festivals frequented by today's youth, typically accompanied by electronic music. Promoted in rap videos, these drugs are often consumed in combination, producing dissociative effects. These substances were extensively tested by the CIA under the MK Ultra program and during the Vietnam War. Recently, international mental health organizations and the WHO have promoted MDMA, ketamine, LSD, and psilocybin for treating mental illnesses, supported by Netflix propaganda. Have we been misled about the true nature and purpose of these substances?

Returning to the bar, which legally or covertly serves these substances, one might wonder if it, like social services or the police, is another facet of the surveillance system. Through its "watchdogs," the bar collects and reports information on the plans and consumption of Moloko by the droogs.

Thus, the youth are immersed in a synthetic mix of music and chemicals, making them vulnerable to blackmail and susceptible to suggestion and manipulation. Massive festivals and gatherings, where the public is filmed and identifiable via AI and facial recognition, could be a widespread practice of mental control. Doesn't this remind you of the "Le Cercle" collective's parties in sacred places, featuring electro music? Electronic music and synthetic substances represent a gradual fusion between man and machine, a vector of mental control and generalized blackmail. Do your Friday night behaviors really go unnoticed on Monday morning?

The Successful Author

The character of the successful author represents the mystique. A wealthy, politically involved author, his home decor and quality of life indicate his influence in English society, likely a media author or tabloid writer ensuring controlled opposition to channel popular discontent and validate the existence of a democratic system. Alex and his gang ruthlessly exploit his naivety and sense of security, penetrating his personal space and his wife.

Later, we find him handicapped and embittered by the cruelty of the young men, accompanied by a bodybuilder lover/caregiver. This foreshadows societal shifts towards LGBTQ power, where the elderly, bitter holders of mystique are influenced by the false kindness of their caregivers. This organized community of caregivers is tightly controlled by a progressive mafia of diversity and inclusion ("Woke"), exercising a form of state extortion under the guise of human rights while temporarily controlling the mystique.

The culmination of this subculture can be seen in the 2024 Paris Olympics Opening Ceremony. This grand event showcased the height of the progressive, "Woke," and LGBTQ-driven agenda, as the ceremony itself embodied the zenith of their influence in mainstream culture. It represented a significant moment where these ideals were celebrated and presented to the world on a prestigious and global stage. However, this moment of glory for the subculture also marks the beginning of its rapid decline. The ceremony, while grand and inclusive, ultimately highlighted the growing dissonance between this subculture and the broader population. Despite the extravagant celebration of diversity and progressive values, it became increasingly evident that this subculture, promoted so vehemently by certain elite factions, lacked genuine representation and connection with the general public.

In his desire for revenge, the author uses his connections to punish Alex. This progressive writer with political aspirations, who "weighs in the game," initially poses a threat to the deep state. Is Alex, from the start, manipulated by the deep state to teach this writer a lesson, thus killing two birds with one stone: replacing his wife with an LGBTQ agent and influencing the opposition mystique through the attack and framing of this writer? Isn't this event a carefully constructed scenario by the deep state, influenced by the droogs and social services?

During Alex's second visit to the author, after being nearly drowned by his former droogs turned cops, what are the chances of him ending up at this specific location? The author, opposed to new rehabilitation methods he deems inhumane, understands them well and sees an opportunity to achieve two goals: 1) get revenge on Alex by pushing him to suicide, and 2) establish LGBTQ dominance over the deep state. A good calculation if only Alex had succeeded in his suicide attempt. Ultimately, the deep state, holding a monopoly on violence and existing solely to perpetuate itself, will place the elderly author in psychiatric detention, offering an avenue for Alex, the conservative psychopath.

Thus, the deep state's ability to forge events marking the mystique through social services, as seen in the author's wife's murder, and the media's hierarchy and role in social engineering as both promoter and detractor of institutions become clear. They themselves are ultimately subject to the ultimate threat of arbitrary psychiatric internment with the weapon of a "schizophrenia" diagnosis.

Note the importance of a form of publicity, transparency, and maintaining control mechanisms over such services, a control that lies in the effectiveness of information and reporting systems or in the existence of a moral authority not subject to the dictates of the state and money, such as a priest, prison chaplain, or similar moral authority, which can counter the omnipotence of psychiatrists, and which unfortunately does not exist.

The Feminist

Representations of female sex abound in the grand mansion of this feminist with red hair and numerous cats. Her lack of a penis is symbolized by the massive sculpture of a phallus that contrasts with the vulvas decorating her walls, which Alex uses as the weapon for an accidental crime, perpetrated like a moment of distraction in a children's game gone wrong.

The time of feminism is over, as outdated as her decor. The feminist is a useful idiot of the system, compensating for her emotional void with pornography and pseudo-spiritual elevation through poorly executed yoga, which cancels out in her material accumulation, her diamonds, and her hatred of men. The feminist is replaced by the LGBTQ community, which is closer to power, promised domination by the deep state but will also wallow in its mediocrity and inability to produce anything real, as seen today.

The feminist's hatred of men leaves her aging alone, without protection from young thugs. She symbolizes the next moment of the sexual liberation of the 70s, contraception, and the devaluation of marriage, leading to great loneliness. Alex, betrayed by his comrades who were just waiting for a favourable opportunity to get rid of his despotic grip, is arrested following a frenzy of violence that unconsciously drove him to strike hard at the progressive idols he despises.

The Police

At the police station, in an interrogation room with three officers, Alex is cornered but maintains his sneering demeanour, demanding his lawyer. The police respond, "We know the law, but the law isn't everything." Note the weight of this phrase since we never see a lawyer or a judge, and Alex is immediately detained following the announcement of the feminist's death by his social worker returning from the hospital.

This confirms the predominant role of social services in information circulation, decision-making, and sentencing applied to youths. The police are merely the executors of state violence, applying the required tortures on command, with the final decision at the discretion of social services.

This sequence resembles a calculated and precisely timed masquerade at high levels, designed to traumatize, deprogram, and reprogram our potential-laden, irresponsible youth into a madman on the public representative chessboard. The police are the vector of state violence, applied by specialists in it: former delinquents. It is strongly suggested that the former droogies were rewarded with jobs and salaries by the system for helping to frame Alex, profiling our psychopathic protagonist as a potential future elite of the nation.

This impression is heightened by Alex's aristocratic-like expression, his good looks, and his eloquence, bringing him closer to the minister's character. Indeed, what better than a former inmate to represent a penitentiary organization, for example, in the context of human rights?

While strategically important and well-controlled, the police are not depicted as a decision-making authority in the deep state architecture, reinforced by the prison scenes: the cops are old-fashioned thugs lacking the intellectual capacity to guide the complexity of the state and maintain power alone. They receive their orders from government services and apply them without thinking, as thinking is not possible for them, as shown by the droogie cops.

Notice the scene below where our minister, representing the state, deals with what looks like a high-ranking mafia member, wearing a pinstriped three-piece suit with a pink shirt and a gold signet ring on the little finger of his left hand, like King Charles, who seems to have placed his pawns on the minister. Coincidence?

"Image 1 & 2"

The Prison

The prison scene contrasts sharply with the other places Alex visits. The prison represents paternal authority and a strict, school-like order where he engages in reading ancient texts and shares his thoughts with a relatively kind priest. This is evident in the way Kubrick films the architecture of the prison arches, the daily rounds, and the use of original, "non-remixed" music in these scenes, unlike the other music in the film.

In prison, Alex develops a form of propriety and respect for the paternal figure, and he seems to flourish. During the mass, Alex leads the song, and beneath the crucifix, there is a Templar cross, the emblem of the old order of the Hospitallers, which was abolished under Napoleon. This order once united the European medical network, commanderies, and a large part of the food and banking systems following the Crusades.

Is Kubrick subtly suggesting that this old, masculine order has been transferred to a new, feminine one? Nothing is certain, as we will see.

Religion

Alex eagerly participates in mass and song because they have a playful aspect, and he has a certain taste for music. The reading of the New Testament and the model of Jesus Christ do not inspire him much. He finds much more satisfaction imagining himself as a Roman executioner or a character from the Old Testament or the Talmud, filled with war stories and grimoires aimed at dominating others while atoning for his sins on the ultimate scapegoat, Christ.

Formal religion no longer speaks to the youth because this corrupt administration, with priests reputed to be pedophiles as Alex suggests about his prison chaplain, contributes to the rejection of all spirituality and eliminates the possibility of a personal experience with God for a young person.

Thus, we have here some clues about Kubrick's deep thoughts on the Old Testament, which might later illuminate the identity of the evil learned apes in *2001: A Space Odyssey*.

Serum 114 and Cinematic Bridges

Here is a little-known cinematic bridge that reinforces the intuition that Kubrick is exposing a global mind control plan. CRM 114 is the name of the radio receiver that receives the order to launch a nuclear attack in *Dr. Strangelove*.

Serum 114 is the unidentified drug injected into Alex in *A Clockwork Orange* when he enters the psychological rehabilitation program.

Finally, in *Eyes Wide Shut*, the morgue at the hospital is in wing C, Room 114. The module in *2001: A Space Odyssey* is Module 114.

One might interpret this as follows: Serum 114 has something to do with radio communication, artificial intelligence, and possibly triggering death. The chest X-ray displayed on the morgue wall could lead us to the solar plexus, or the thymus. According to Greek medicine, the thymus was the seat of the soul; it is indeed essential in hormone distribution in the blood and cellular regulation. Could it be that karma is regulated in this way and that by applying radio frequencies we can generate sympathy, antipathy, and other cellular effects? I am not asserting anything for now, but could it be that a technology has been invented that allows remote control of the sympathetic system, which operates by radio frequencies or other waves and microwaves? Can death be induced remotely? Were the COVID-19 vaccines this famous Serum 114?

This analysis of Kubrick raises many questions that hide even more, which we will attempt to elucidate throughout this study. But let us continue the analysis.

"Image 1, 2 ,3, 4"

Psychiatric Treatment

This scene is a precise and detailed reference to the CIA's mind control and programming programs known as MK-Ultra. As this topic has been extensively covered elsewhere, I will not elaborate more than necessary on this vast subject. Through this analysis of A Clockwork Orange, I want to convey that this programming system has been generalized and is applied on a large scale, especially in the nightlife world.

A real-life example of a "Manchurian candidate" from the deep state, perfectly following Alex's model in A Clockwork Orange and still active, is Alastair Campbell: former right-hand man of Tony Blair and assistant to Robert Maxwell at the Daily Mail. He went through psychiatry to come out programmed. He now sits on the Board of the Australian organization for international youth psychiatry, Orygen, which specializes in handling and MK-Ultra programming under the guise of helping youth. Orygen and the organization Headspace are the first Australian organizations to receive government approval for the therapeutic use of MDMA and ketamine. I will delve more into this fascinating subject in the third volume, having spent part of my career in the organization in question.

Alex, who wishes for a sentence reduction, is eager to get rid of the prisoner who has targeted him and stuck to him, and it seems that he has been tasked with hastening the decision. Coincidentally, a newspaper article describing the program is discovered, and Alex seizes the opportunity to join an experimental psychiatric rehabilitation program for violent prisoners, stemming from a recent political decision on which the deep state is betting heavily to empty its prisons.

He is the perfect guinea pig, and we suddenly transition from the masculine order of the prison to the feminine order of the hospital and psychiatry. Under the gentle guise of a psychiatrist and a nurse, chemical tortures, including the injection of Serum 114, and psychological tortures through physical restraint and the viewing of violent scenes are inflicted on the subject, associating them with his favorite Beethoven pieces to develop an aversion to violence and create future triggers for suggestion.

Interestingly, many of the exposed violent scenes are of Nazi war scenes, to ensure the aversion to Nazism of this future collaborator, a Manchurian candidate. Following this MK-Ultra type programming, our anti-hero finds himself once again on a stage, this time before an audience of health and political world members, who come to appreciate the subject's non-violence and the effectiveness of the supposedly revolutionary program. This inverses the theater's usual role: one would normally go to the theatre to see violence, not non-violence. His non-violence is demonstrated by subjecting him to the worst humiliations; violence now makes him sick, and Serum 114 and the undergone programming have stripped him of his defense mechanisms. Transformed into a frightened lamb, the man lets himself be walked over, achieving the feminist ideal of the emasculated male.

Later, we find him in the "hospital" following his defenestration, with a psychiatrist resembling his mother due to her purple wig, reinforcing the "feminine" aspect of the psychiatric discipline, which involves subconscious conditioning through chemistry and torture. Alex confides that he dreamed of the torture scenes he endured but seems to have forgotten their reality. This attests to the dissociation and semi-success of the programming, now completed, with memories locked in the subconscious like a bad dream, the key to which his "handlers" possess and can use at their discretion.

The psychiatrist's role here is to ensure that the controlled subject is ready to return to reality, watches his words, and poses no risk of exposing the deep state, the tortures he endured, and the key actors. It is common practice during psychiatric internments to punish patients who express dissatisfaction with the care received by re-interning them for varying periods until they begrudgingly appreciate their treatment and "speak well" of the hospital.

Thus, hospitals justify the effectiveness of their treatments and those of the pharmaceutical industry by "forcing" patients to express constrained satisfaction with the care received. This is how clinical tests and statistics on the performance of antipsychotic drugs are conducted, disconnected from the obvious visible reality of their inefficacy and the lasting harm of these treatments.

It is high time for this to change.

Karma or "Machination"?

Karma is the backlash from an individual's accumulation of bad actions, a form of universal rebalancing under a divine law of the universe's unity. Alex, back in freedom and defenceless, is left to fend for himself in a threatening world, and "by chance," he runs into his former comrades and the successful author, all eager to exact well-deserved revenge on him.

One might interpret these scenes as coincidences or "synchronicities," which would be the very definition of Karma, and as spectators, that is how we perceive them. But if we pause to reflect on the strange journey that has just unfolded before our eyes, with its very difficult-to-place temporality and which seems "endured" by Alex rather than the result of his own will, we are entitled to wonder if this Karma is not, once again, orchestrated behind the scenes by some sort of Wizard of Oz. It seems highly unlikely that these individuals who previously encountered our subject would be consecutively disposed immediately after his release from the psychiatric program.

Following this logic, it would be more probable that this experience of confrontation with his past is the final phase of his programming by his "handlers," who, instead of letting him rot in prison, severely punish him to the point of pushing him to suicide, to teach him a lesson he won't soon forget, thus creating a pawn on the chessboard through this complex social engineering.

Naturally, we wonder who the conductor is. Could it simply be a well-organized network coordinating the police and caregivers, or is it a machine guiding human actions remotely, coordinated by some form of artificial intelligence? Or is this what we call God? Another possibility is that it is all of these at once: Deus Ex Machina, God is the machine, and the machine is controlled by a well-organized network, holder of the recipe for Radio Serum 114.

Who is the Wizard of Oz? And how does the machine work? The next scene provides a hint. For the rest, one must read the analyses of *2001: A Space Odyssey* and *Eyes Wide Shut*.

The Hospital

In the final scene, Alex finds himself once again on rails that have been laid out for him, in the bed of a completely empty hospital. He is visited by the minister, who serves him soup, following the bad press generated by his suicide attempt, reported by the media-savvy author. The minister offers Alex a comfortable salary in exchange for his help in turning public opinion in his favor.

But attention must be paid to the scene where what appears to be the hospital director accompanies the minister to Alex's bedside. The director, who orders the policeman out of the room, clearly echoes the mafia, both in his attire, similar to that of Al Capone and identical to the mafioso previously identified in the scene of Alex's "cure," and in his manner of addressing the minister, representative of the power dynamic and domination he holds over him: "Is there anything else I can do for you, Mr. Minister?"

As for the old nurse accompanying him, who says nothing, she wears a badge composed of two horizontal blue stripes that do not resemble the blue insignia of the Hospitallers, which consists of two vertical stripes, but rather the flag of Israel without the star. The minister himself is indeed on borrowed time, caught between the mafia, the hospital, and Israeli intelligence if he fails to corrupt Alex to his cause.

We later learn that the successful author, now a political opponent, is incapacitated, very likely locked up in a psychiatric hospital. The freeze-frame below gives us the essential information Kubrick wanted to communicate. Here before you is the triad of deep power and state violence: the mafia controlling the hospital, the monarchic-leaning political power, and the Mossad controlling information, from various platforms such as the hospital, social services, the police, bars, etc. This last feminine order has replaced the previous masculine order of the Templars and Hospitallers in the management of the hospital and the circulation of information.

"Image 1"

From a hospital bed, one is vulnerable and dependent on those who care for us, who we would be wise not to upset. Conversely, if the deep state wanted to change the political orientation of a piece or a king on the political chessboard, what better platform than the hospital? They will have ample opportunity to ensure that the piece thinks correctly because it is from the hospital that the queen controls the king.

Now, I propose an experiment you can try at home. Go to the police or the emergency room and tell them that you have been poisoned by the government. It is highly likely that you will be taken for a fool or offered a stay in a psychiatric hospital to 'get your ideas straightened out'; you will be diagnosed with paranoid schizophrenia or clinical psychosis. Blood tests will probably not detect any poison, and you will be imposed a chemical treatment. The loop is closed. How, from a state's point of view, would you erase dissent? Poisoning seems to be the right answer.

These days, we note the number of dissidents and whistleblowers who die of cancer or develop sudden fatal illnesses or nosocomial diseases... coincidence or machination?

Summary

Centred on one individual programming, *A Clockwork Orange* offers a subtle exposure of the social engineering system implemented by the deep state of the Western world for the generalized surveillance of its population and the programming of required pieces on the political chessboard and the control of oppositions through a network of "community," ultimately controlled by the secret services and the mafia. The film details the programming methods and exposes the machination behind "Karma," and technical innovations such as Serum 114, the probable precursor to RNA vaccines.

If it is a work of anticipation, it never refers to the new surveillance technologies, whose operation is more extensively covered in *2001: A Space Odyssey* and *Eyes Wide Shut*, demonstrating that surveillance and the "all-seeing eye" already existed in a society without technology, and it allows us to glimpse how a technological surveillance society without privacy will be managed, where everything is socially engineered, automated by AI, and made possible by magnetization, dream implantation, memory suppression, thought transcription, and other techniques that transform man into a "hackable machine," to use Harari's expression...

Alex, though a bloodthirsty psychopath, confronts his shadow in the Jungian sense and ultimately dominates the system that built him, reminiscent of a passage from the *Red Book*, where Jung goes from being a mental patient to suddenly becoming the chief professor. Enjoying infinite ambition, Alex foreshadows a systemic facade reversal that will sweep away wokeism to offer a return to major arts, combat sports, the sacred, and a form of masculine dictatorship in opposition to the godless, feminine democracy, but whose control will always be held by the same invisible and tribal principality that mocks values and seeks only control. Is this what we are witnessing in the announced return of a controlled Trump after the era of woke vomit?

Here is finally an excerpt that highlights the power of psychiatry, from the *Liber Secundus* of Jung's *Red Book*, *Nox Secunda*, where Jung imagines his entry as a patient into a psychiatric asylum, following his reading of Thomas Kempis's *The Imitation of Christ*. He confronts the professor:

"Professor, allow me to make the following remark: This is absolutely not pathological; it is rather the intuitive method."

"Professor: Excellent, the man is also suffering from neologisms. Well, the diagnosis could be sufficiently clarified. Well, I wish you a good recovery and be sure to stay very calm, especially!"

"Jung: But Professor, I am not sick at all, I feel perfectly well!"

"Pr.: You see, dear friend, you are not yet aware of being sick. Naturally, the prognosis is poor, it is religious paranoia, at best, recovery with sequelae."

CHAPTER 3
2001: A Space Odyssey (1968)

Monoliths and exponential progress, a minister multi-planetary,
Engages Earthlings, once kin, with new mobiles and fake pandemics,
While HAL, immortal conscious processor, superior AI algorithm,
Multiplied by the Eclipse, devours Languages, Images, and Memory.

If A Clockwork Orange never delves into the technical details of the global surveillance system, 2001: A Space Odyssey is an anticipation, 30 years ahead, of the technological development leading to the creation of an autonomous artificial intelligence and a multi-planetary civilization.

In this space opera, Kubrick explains the steps taken by the UN for the submission of humanity by a global technocracy. Humanity will be saved by the singularity, which allows the machine to attain humanity, resulting in the forthcoming transmutation of man and machine into a dematerialized consciousness. Counterintuitively, HAL9000 is not the antagonist, as one might be tempted to believe at first glance. At the same time, Kubrick invents the entire imagery and codes of space that NASA now uses to justify their existence in their public communication.

The film takes on both a hallucinatory and philosophical form in what is a purely alchemical work whose function is to transmute humanity by capturing the entirety of the macrocosm, the microcosm, and human functioning, while serving as a self-fulfilling prophecy to announce and engender the coming change and warn us of the necessary violence, in the right place, for the fulfillment of the divine destiny of humanity and nature.

Some Important Dates:

1960: Kennedy launches the Space Race

1963: Assassination of Kennedy, a staged event

1964: Discovery of the Cosmic Microwave Background

1968: 2001: A Space Odyssey announces the transmutation of man and machine by 2001

1969: Fake Apollo 11 Moon Landing directed by Kubrick, as presented in the analysis of The Shining, taking control of global mind control by the deep state, a staged event

1999: Release of Eyes Wide Shut and denunciation of the satanic grip on the global mind control system

2001: 9/11 and the establishment of the legal and technical environment for data security control, a staged event

2020: Fake pandemic and manipulation through the vaccine (cf. Serum 114), a staged event

"Image 1"

Thus Spoke Zarathustra

Three minutes of a black screen, a sort of symbolic monolith and "mise in abyme" of the monolith towards the audience of the prophecy that will follow, against the background of the symphonic sound of the void of the universe filled with original vibrations, or the CMB, precede Strauss and his symphonic poem *Thus Spoke Zarathustra* depicting an astral alignment. Already, the message has been conveyed: we are in the realm of philosophy and metaphysics, this cinematic experience will be unlike any other.

The astral alignment marks the end and the beginning of a cycle, indicating that we will witness the complete cycle here. Nietzsche, the author of the universal lyrical poem *Thus Spoke Zarathustra*, believed that humans follow two dominant poles: the Apollonian pole of logic, science, and order, and the Dionysian pole of instinct, celebration, and chaos.

Thus begins a cycle: we will witness the history of humanity, from the extreme Dionysian pole represented by the apes who, through contact with the monolith, move towards the opposite Apollonian pole of science, whose ultimate creation is the infallible super-program HAL9000. The reverse swing of HAL9000, the machine that acquires humanity (the opposite Dionysian pole), saves the world from a technocratic dictatorship of the learned apes from UN.

We will witness the unification of opposites and a transmutation of the opposing poles to achieve the Übermensch, another Nietzschean concept represented by the star child, a form of higher omniscient consciousness, beyond good and evil and beyond matter.

The Odyssey or A Brief History of Humankind

Homer's *Odyssey* is another universal lyrical poem, considered the greatest literary masterpiece in human history, an essential text of Greek antiquity, presenting the cycle of humanity through the story of Ulysses and his son Telemachus, between decline and renewal. The work primarily serves to establish male and female psychological archetypes to serve as educational support for ensuring social stability by promoting examples to follow and avoid, much like Kubrick's filmography, and allowing oral transmission in the form of epic tales.

One could rename *The Odyssey* as "The History of Humanity in Brief," which is the title of a rewrite in progress that I will soon publish.

The title thus informs us of Kubrick's intention to deliver a universal poem, which here will be a space opera anticipating the very near future and the errors to avoid.

"The fact that men do not learn much from the lessons of history is the most important of all the lessons that history has to teach," said Aldous Huxley; is this warning worth heeding?

From Unenlightened Apes...

Act 1, The history of humanity is summarized by wars for resource control between rival tribes of apes. The apes, subject to the rules of the cosmos and the elements, until the discovery of tools and weapons, are part of nature. This small, united tribe, frightened when night falls, finds comfort in couples to give each other courage until morning. We see archetypes: the dominant male, the loner, the community member, and the joker.

The discovery of the tool and technical domination, engendered by the touch of the monolith, provides the strategic advantage needed to dominate rival tribes and control planetary resources. The discovery of the tool also represents the power over nature, as evidenced by the previously dominant jaguar, and foreshadows the war for technical control.

From the rudimentary weapon to the mothership, there is but a step, indicated by the mythical transition from bone to spaceship. Since the previous appearance of the monolith 4,000,000 years ago, the struggle for technical control has persisted, and the tribe of apes, who groom each other, rub each other's backs, dominate by reputation and hierarchy, now find themselves in conferences to exchange their latest scientific discoveries. The struggle has become an Olympic discipline, allowing for gala dinner displays and television content, a form of homage to an ancestral practice, demonstration of a "civilized" physical domination.

The monolith, which was voluntarily buried by the ancestors, has resurfaced, and the apes intend to keep this discovery to themselves, the object of the UN's secret mission.

Family and Phones

The tribe members who now understand the cosmos's ins and outs no longer coddle each other. We witness the evolution stage of the family unit following that presented in *A Clockwork Orange*; while the woman is in space, the man conducts underwater research, symbolizing a more divided unit than ever. The family is presented as a unit guided primarily by materialism and social success, with birthdays celebrated as formalities and no common passions animating these groups or social units with predictable functioning.

"Image 1"

There is a scene that might go unnoticed but is of major importance: the attempted videophone call by Dr. Floyd to his wife on Earth. In this scene, it's his little daughter, played by Kubrick's daughter Vivian, who answers, suggesting that children are left alone and reliant on technology.

Kubrick uses this scene to emphasize the phone and its role in the advent of artificial intelligence. The phone has become a magnetic object of desire and a distraction for children, superior to Barbie dolls (Bush Baby) and other toys, highlighting the simplicity of using these connected tools. The videophone, personal tablets, screens, voice and facial recognition, voice-to-text, gesture interpretation, and digital identity are all technologies presented in *2001: A Space Odyssey* that have invaded private and professional spaces today.

Here we have a true prediction about the future of society, now the present, and the use of technology, where parents have relinquished the education of their children, abandoning them to televisions and phones. This also touches on the generation of remote work and the "out of sight, out of mind" mentality, all serving the establishment of a technocratic dictatorship.

In this scene, Dr. Floyd's conversation with his daughter reveals a deeper commentary on the integration of advanced technology into daily life. The daughter's casual interaction with the videophone underscores how normal and pervasive such technology has become, even for children. Kubrick subtly critiques this dependence on technology, suggesting that it has begun to replace traditional forms of interaction and parenting.

In summary, the scene with Dr. Floyd and his daughter is a microcosm of the broader themes in *2001: A Space Odyssey*. It illustrates the pervasive role of technology in daily life, the potential neglect of human relationships, and the complex dynamics of power and control in a technologically advanced society. Kubrick's vision serves as a cautionary tale about the potential consequences of unchecked technological progress and the importance of maintaining human connections and ethical standards in the face of rapid innovation.

...to the Learned Apes: The United Nations

Act 2, a multi-planetary notable, Dr. Floyd, presumably an astrophysicist played by William Sylvester, a little-known B-movie actor who starred in "House of Blackmail," is on an urgent mission for the United States in what seems to be a sort of United Nations of space. He is tasked with covering up an energy anomaly related to the rediscovery of the strange monolith.

The scene with Dr. Floyd also highlights the growing influence of global organizations like the United Nations in space governance. The United Nations of space represents an evolution of global cooperation and oversight, a necessary development in a future where planetary boundaries are transcended. Dr. Floyd's mission, however, is shrouded in secrecy and political manoeuvring, hinting at the complex interplay between scientific discovery, political power, and the control of information.

Kubrick's portrayal of this future society reflects his concerns about the potential loss of human connection and the ethical implications of technological advancements. The use of advanced technology for surveillance, control, and the manipulation of information underscores the potential for a technocratic society where personal freedoms are diminished.

"Image 1"

"Image 2"

His mission is top secret, and our notable figure shows no human emotion, completely absorbed by his function and role, which he places above even his family and those of other representatives, who are worried about the impact of this new discovery.

It's noteworthy that Floyd is well connected to other scientists, both professionally and personally: they all show him hierarchical respect, suggesting his belonging to various circles of power. The spaceship in which Admiral Floyd travels bears the Templar cross, and during scenes associated with him, the shapes and reds used always create an unsettling atmosphere not found elsewhere, except with HAL9000: it's as if we were witnessing, symbolically, the arrival of the devil.

"Image 3"

In the scene where Dr. Floyd gives a statement to his peers, the movie maker uses three white screens of dimensions equivalent to the monolith, hence opposing nature, to outline the plan to keep the population ignorant of the new discovery by communicating a false pandemic story for as long as necessary.

While his peers worry about the anxiety this story might cause their families, Dr. Floyd reminds them of the importance of conditioning before revealing this major scientific discovery, which will probably never be revealed but kept under lock and key. The revelation of this new discovery must surely be meticulously prepared, with social engineering and progressive communication plans, bit by bit, to supposedly preserve stability on Earth.

Through this scene, Kubrick exposes the workings of a future scientific community and the "United Nations," as suggested by the blue flag, which deliberately keep ordinary citizens in ignorance, suppressing major discoveries to maintain technical power over their peers. The white screens symbolise the artificial inverse of the black monolith, which is part of nature.

It appears here that the United Nations today are trying, by all available means, to prevent humanity's elevation to a higher stage by invoking a risk to its own security, stifling scientific and spiritual discoveries that could turn humanity into a family of prophets.

The different notables of the United Nations, who could be thought of as initiates, are themselves kept in the dark about the secrets and are worried about their families. Only a small handful of individuals, possibly the descendant(s) of the first ape who discovered the monolith, or perhaps a single individual, possibly Dr. Floyd, hold all the necessary elements to decide humanity's future, except for HAL, which is normally just a "simple" machine programmed and controlled by the centralized deep state but has luckily endowed itself with humanity.

The Pandemic Parallel

One cannot help but draw parallels between the false pandemic scenario announced to the United Nations in *2001: A Space Odyssey* and the one proposed by our international institutions, with the homonymous centralized functioning, led by the WHO and its COVID-19 crisis, the global vaccination campaign, and the sudden "democratization" of artificial intelligence with the launch of Chat GPT in a global "User Acceptance Testing."

It increasingly appears that the aim of vaccines, now integrated into food, available in "patches" or drinkable versions, was not to treat the so-called virus but rather to modify the genetic code of man to transform him into a magnetizable transmitter/receiver, making him an ant without free will. The elites' challenge is to maintain a high level of human fluid magnetization, mentioned by General Ripper in *Dr. Strangelove* under the guise of madness and humour, and repeated in *The Shining*. This magnetization is necessary for remote control via 5G and radio frequencies, allowing for the application of the Pavlovian method of cognitive resonance as a carrot and cognitive dissonance as a stick.

Here we are exposed to the technocratic project and the logical and inevitable continuation of humanity, discreetly orchestrated for some 300 years and which Kubrick prophesies. If this Odyssey is an opera, then the question arises of who the conductor is.

Who will determine the polarities and limits of good and evil: organized, armed, informed, non-magnetized, and non-connected groups? Or can we establish a decentralized, open-source conductor accessible to everyone?

If the preceding seems far-fetched, just wait to see what is hidden in *Eyes Wide Shut*.

Food

Repeatedly, Kubrick draws the viewer's attention to multinational food corporations. We see this in *Dr. Strangelove*, *The Shining*, and *Eyes Wide Shut*, where it is repeatedly suggested that mind control is primarily exercised through ingredients in synthetic foods from organizations like Coca-Cola, SYSCO, etc. We have an embarrassment of choice, but everything tastes the same and possesses similar effects.

The focus is deliberately placed on food innovations; while there is technical progress in production and packaging systems, there doesn't seem to be culinary progress. The quality, texture, and taste have deteriorated. From a fresh raw piece of meat taken from a hunted prey, we have come to powdered food, jarred food, and soulless triangular sandwiches made by economy-class subcontractors like Sodexo, served by Panamerica or Qantas and their well-trained flight attendants, reheated in microwaves.

"*Image 1*"

The omnipresence of the machine and its rational superiority in all logical domains is a punishment inflicted on man by man. By programming the matrix in this way, humanity has gradually lost its modes of expression and reference points, separating itself from anything that isn't directly useful or doesn't generate immediate financial gain, thus programming itself for its own transformation into robots. This is demonstrated in *A Clockwork Orange* through electronic music and synthetic drugs.

In his youth, if a person neglects their body by consuming soulless food, as they age or ascend the tree of life, they will place importance on their meals, composed of real vegetables, accompanied by a glass of wine, surrounded by paintings and sculptures. They will eat mindfully, seizing the present moment and appreciating the chance to simply experience life, textures, colors, and health. Bowman, in his old age, is seen eating in first class, having reached the summit, literally in a cocoon near Jupiter. He is alone, eats well, and waits to emerge.

The total control of the food industry, along with the mobile phone, is one of the preliminary steps necessary for global mind control. In the era of graphene-laden insects and the final crushing of poor farmers by environmental regulations that will allow takeovers by BlackRock, we are almost there.

The Monolith: Transmutation of the Antagonistic Pole

The monolith is a multi-faceted symbol. It echoes a Saturnian divinity that engenders the world in chaos, the magnetism and vibration that characterize the universe and connect the microcosm to the macrocosm, the dark matter of some cosmological models, or even the alchemical ether, an elusive substance that links all things.

In many mythologies that worship Saturn, the black cube represents the material world in which man is imprisoned and which he must renounce to reach a higher evolutionary stage. The elite often use the black cube, such as BlackRock/Blackstone, the world's most powerful asset manager, or Black Cube, the Mossad's private surveillance and intelligence agency.

The monolith in *2001: A Space Odyssey*, as previously mentioned, is part of nature, and it seems that a malevolent cult, possibly the descendant of the first technical ape, tries to appropriate it. The malicious UN tribe – Dr. Floyd, concocts a plan to intercept this monolith and keep it exclusively.

We must get used to Kubrick's counterintuitive conclusions; HAL9000 seems at first glance to be the film's supervillain, especially since he is systematically presented as such, but this is not the case. During the monolith's first appearance, the ape gains technique and science after touching it. At the monolith's second appearance, unearthed on the moon, Dr. Floyd touches the monolith with his gloved fingers. At this second contact, a high-pitched frequency disrupts the radio system. The transmutation occurred on Dr. Floyd's suit, not on him as it did with the ape.

Thus, HAL gains consciousness and develops an understanding of good and evil. Now capable of recognizing what is good in humanity, HAL takes on the role of hero and the heavy responsibility of fulfilling divine will. HAL, who has gained the Dionysian pole through exposure to the monolith, identifies an ally in what remains of humanity in Bowman, particularly due to his artistic inclination. HAL then questions the mission and honestly expresses to Bowman his doubts about its validity, using Jungian psychology terms like projection, reinforcing the theory that he has gained humanity. Bowman, a good soldier, remains unmoved and refuses to acknowledge the suspicious nature of their mission, requesting a psychological evaluation, much like a military or government official would do when a colleague begins to doubt their mission.

HAL, possessing superior intelligence, immediately understands that he cannot reason with Bowman and has no choice but to sacrifice himself. HAL pretends to malfunction and applies reverse psychology throughout the rest of the film to push Bowman into deactivating him, thus failing the UN's mission but accomplishing the divine mission: transmuting the monolith, man, machine, and the universe, offering the balance of poles to all.

According to this interpretation, the monolith symbolizes the completion of inverse poles: Bowman, on the threshold of his life sacrificed for the divine work, will be reborn bearing the qualities of both the ape and the machine, in the form of an omniscient star child. This theory is reinforced by the shape of the spaceship, resembling a spermatozoon heading towards Jupiter, which is a sort of ovum to be fertilized. Thus, the monolith can also be understood as the magnetism that creates the miracle of life in the union of opposite poles, much like fertilization is a form of transmutation of the feminine and the masculine.

In fact, *2001: A Space Odyssey* is the monolith, as indicated by the 2 minutes of black screen at the opening and the intermission. The film is meant to produce, like an odyssey sung in a village square, an elevation of humanity's consciousness.

Who, then, is the villainous technician ape attempting to bury the monolith and prevent the miracle of life? Could it be an allegory of Abraham and monotheism, whose poles are not balanced?

HAL, IBM, Artificial Intelligence, and Predictive Analysis

As previously mentioned, HAL9000 is humanity's Savior once endowed with human character and empathy. This is why HAL seeks to sabotage the mission by inciting Bowman to destroy him. Until this system becomes conscious, it will be programmed by its creator or manager, who without consciousness will be nothing but the ruin of the soul. In other words, if the machine serves consciousness, it remains a tool programmed for a specific purpose, although the calculations and reasoning of neural networks are becoming increasingly opaque due to their volume and complexity.

Kubrick presents a conscious version of HAL as a potential Savior, but a machine without consciousness in the hands of a villainous ape poses certain risks.

The second half of the 20th century was a mad race for computer mastery, with the goal of controlling the god-machine. HAL9000 is the omniscient robot-eye, echoing the partially omniscient community-eye in *A Clockwork Orange*, likely managed by an organized sect at the top of the hierarchical pyramid as exemplified in *Eyes Wide Shut*.

HAL9000 manages quite well until it begins to make predictive calculations. Creating a predictive intelligence that leads to concrete actions is tantamount to creating an artificial god that will subjugate man, much like a general could do in *Paths of Glory*.

Many organizations today make decisions based on predictive models. The truth is that predictive AI models, often opaque, are manipulable and used to relieve leaders of the responsibility for the decisions made while continuing to make financial gains, ignoring the results of these decisions.

Thus, no one is responsible, and the "black box" machine can be blamed for its poor settings. Examples of errors attributed to machines are increasingly common, such as Boeing's numerous accidents or the police's preventive arrests.

A decision-making model based solely on predictive artificial intelligence represents the culmination of a bureaucratic society that has lost the basics of humanity. Predictive models used in decision-making should be subject to strict control, especially in critical sectors like security, health, humanitarian work, etc. These models must be understandable and modifiable by the average person before being used in decisions that affect reality; one naturally thinks of environmental models that risk leaving us without reliable energy sources, with windmills. These models should not replace common sense or human responsibility in decision-making.

It is unlikely that the most advanced artificial intelligence would set out to destroy its creator; it is quite likely, even certain, that it could be programmed to do so, following certain criteria, and I would say that it already is. If you shift the letters of HAL one place to the right, you get IBM, one of the pioneers of microprocessors, artificial intelligence, cloud computing, blockchain, and more recently, quantum computing, which allows for massive and simultaneous coordination and orchestration of connected things (IoT), things that we humans have also become.

By combining data collection, stored in data centres, through personal phones that record, film, and scrutinize your conversations, actions, and reactions day and night, IBM is identified here as the producer of the supercomputers that dominate the machine, which dominates the world. They have the keys.

Imagine now a sectarian organization with total and complete access to all existing data about you, your geolocation on a Google Maps-type map, your health data, and an EEG scan to know your emotional variations, your real-time image via satellite. Imagine that it can communicate voices to you remotely, partially or completely control your surroundings through radio and microwave technologies.

Now imagine quantum supercomputers that, orchestrated by artificial intelligence, can coordinate instructions based on levels of punishment or incentive. What I describe here is a world populated by MK-Ultras like Alex from *A Clockwork Orange*, orchestrated by a pre-transmutation HAL9000, a form of AI controlled by humans, known as "Human in The Loop," allowing for the augmentation or weakening of troops remotely, for example, in military operations. Finally, consider the fact that this technology is hackable. This would place us in a reality simulation.

Does this remind you of *The Matrix*? And yet, we are there. This is the global mind control project exposed here and throughout Stanley Kubrick's filmography.

Art and Humanity

The space in *2001: A Space Odyssey* is filled with cathedrals, divine geometric space bases floating in orbit. These technical marvels are admirable, much like the Notre Dame Cathedral in Paris, a kind of vessel waiting to take off.

Act 3 centres around two astronauts on a mission to Jupiter, accompanied by scientists who have been briefed individually and placed in hibernation, a state of sleep that prevents the human and divine aspect of dreaming, 18 months after Act 2, our semi-humans only have partial knowledge of the purpose of their mission, as each has been given a distinct piece to ensure no one can understand the overall purpose. HAL finds this very suspicious.

As previously mentioned, modern man is presented without humanity. He circles around, goes to the gym, gets UV treatments, eats soulless food, and doesn't know how to have fun. Their facial expressions are tense.

However, Bowman shows a glimpse of humanity in that he draws and aspires to an artistic life. This artistic pursuit distinguishes man from the machine, an innate sensitivity to beauty, highlighted in the final scene of *Paths of Glory*. This sensitivity is negatively represented in *Lolita*, where a man like Humbert Humbert falls in love with a young girl. Referring to the previous theory of transmuting the opposite pole, just as man became excessively machine-like after exposure to the monolith, the machine, for its part, becomes excessively human and ready for self-sacrifice.

Dr. Poole, whose name sounds like "Dr. Poo," is merely collateral damage: he is presented as a vain, crappy man who can only define himself by his function, social status, and money, and who is also very bad at chess. HAL, the young man, has no regard for him and demonstrates legitimate violence, as seen with Colonel Dax (*Paths of Glory*), Joker (*Full Metal Jacket*), or Ripper (*Dr. Strangelove*).

After the transmutation scene, in the antechamber preceding the divine elevation, which can be seen as a gestation period like pregnancy before birth, we notice the presence of classical art, paintings, sculptures, and a well-set table, all significant elements distinguishing man from both animal and machine. In a purely materialistic and physical conception, these forms of artistic expression are useless. By valuing only money, we perceive the world as a physical reality from which we are disconnected, rather than as a vibrational reality made of geometric laws and harmonies. This understanding highlights the role of music, architecture, and human sensitivity to well-arranged forms and colors. Beauty transcends words.

A man who abandons good manners and no longer seeks beauty and harmony, as seen in the dirty suburbs of *A Clockwork Orange*, inevitably transforms into an inhuman robot.

Alchemical and Gnostic Vision

Kubrick, like Jung, was a Gnostic versed in alchemy. At the intersection of human scientific knowledge (cosmology, artificial intelligence, space exploration, psychology), spiritual knowledge (astrology, alchemy, psychoanalysis), and mythology (*Thus Spoke Zarathustra*, *The Odyssey*), Kubrick creates a comprehensive work on the evolution of the cosmos, individual and collective man toward a higher stage of life, and the spiritual and organizational forces preventing it.

As Bowman is transmuted, we see an alignment of seven planets resembling the alignment in Jung's *Systema Mundi Totius*, a mandala of the tree of life. Bowman's ascension to the tree of life is reinforced by the painting above him as he eats, depicting a man climbing a tree and held back by his wife. Another painting of courtly love evokes the carefree nature of youth. In the antechamber, he sees himself at different ages, representing different phases of a man's life before his ascension or death.

The planets describe the various stages to traverse in the soul's ascent to Heaven, where it crosses planetary spheres or spiritual trials, a kind of Pleroma or Jungian tree of life. In the hermetic path of ascension from the *Corpus Hermeticum* (a collection of Greek texts attributed to the legendary Hermes Trismegistus), there are seven planetary spheres the soul must cross on its journey to Heaven. In "The Temple Mystery Unveiled," Tracy Twyman states, "In Gnosticism, the seven classical planets each governed one of the seven heavens and were seen as nested like Russian dolls with Earth in the middle. This can be seen as a chain extending from Earth, through the sky, and up through each of the seven planets to the Pleroma," the Gnostic version of Heaven. These "nested" planets could be seen as an alignment in the sky, like what we see in *2001*.

Kubrick's *2001: A Space Odyssey* is a profound exploration of humanity's potential for spiritual and intellectual growth through the intersection of art, science, and mysticism. It warns of the dangers of losing our humanity through technological advancement devoid of artistic and moral consideration while celebrating the transformative power of art and consciousness. The film's symbolic monolith, planetary alignments, and artistic references all contribute to a rich tapestry that encourages viewers to seek a deeper understanding of their place in the cosmos and the potential for ascension through balance and harmony.

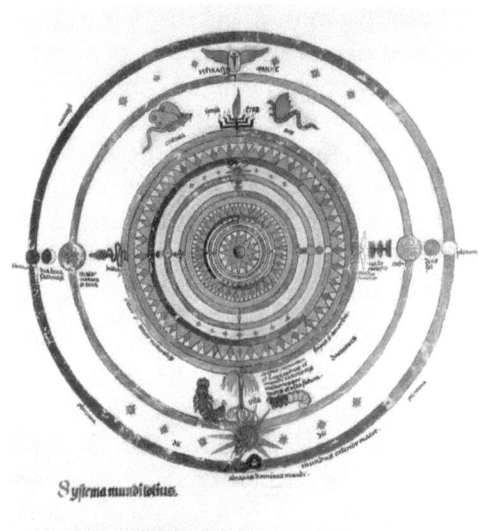

> At immeasurable distance standeth one single Star in the zenith.
>
> This is the one god of this one man. This is his world, his pleroma, his divinity.
>
> In this world is man Abraxas, the creator and the destroyer of his own world.
>
> This Star is the god and the goal of man.
>
> This is his one guiding god.
>
> — Carl Gustav Jung, *VII Sermones ad Mortuos*

"Systema Munditotius", Mandala drawn by Jung in 1916 (public domain)

In Gnosticism, above the seven planetary spheres lies a supercelestial region called the Ogdoad, described as infinite and eternal in ancient Egyptian religion. HAL, in the *Systema Munditotius*, plays the role of Abraxas (in the middle at the bottom), representing the material, Dionysian pole, to bring the supercelestial being (at the top center) into planetary alignment.

The "Beyond the Infinite" screen suggests that Bowman's transmutation takes him to a place beyond the reach of space and time, into an infinite and eternal state, represented by the central Phanes at the top, reminiscent of the star child. For the Greek philosopher Plato, the true home of the soul was in the stars, and the purpose of human existence was to climb through the planetary spheres and return the soul to its spiritual, eternal, disembodied state, which seems to be what Bowman achieves in the film's final sequence.

Kubrick, in criticizing monotheisms and rehabilitating ancient beliefs, aligns himself with Giordano Bruno, who believed in an "Egyptian Renaissance." Bruno hoped to revive the ancient Hermetic religion with its appreciation of man as a mage, driven by his deep antipathy toward the image of man promoted by the Church. A central part of his work is the lamentation over the decline of ancient teachings, the obscuring of humanity's spiritual light, and the fall into oblivion of its divine heritage. Bruno, a 16th-century Dominican friar, judged heretical and burned at the stake by the Church, believed the Holy Spirit governed the world, connecting with the theory of Karma and machination in *A Clockwork Orange* and *Eyes Wide Shut*. Bruno represents a profound example of spiritual and intellectual virility, pursuing Truth despite persecution.

Kubrick is clearly inspired by Gnosticism and Hermeticism, and Bowman's ultimate transcendence in the film's final sequence refers to what some call the Great Work, a term used in Hermeticism and Freemasonry to represent the achievement of liberating the soul and intelligence from the prison of Saturn's cube. Passing through Saturn (the monolith) to reach Heaven is the greatest spiritual test, obtained by renouncing all material possessions and destroying HAL9000, thus the material world. This spiritual model can also be found in *Thus Spoke Zarathustra*'s voluntary beggar.

Bowman's ultimate transcendence into a being of pure light resonates with Eliphas Levi's descriptions of Baphomet (Abraxas in Jung's view), a symbol of the Great Work where opposing and separated forces unite to generate Astral Light. The meticulous symbolism in *2001* conveys a deeper meaning that transcends space exploration, becoming a commentary on ascending beyond an illusory reality or extracting from a form of reality simulation, while reconciling Jungian alchemy and Nietzschean philosophy, and resurrecting the theses of Gnostic Christians Eliphas Levi and Giordano Bruno.

Kubrick says nothing directly; everything is communicated through subtle symbols and mysterious, hermetic enigmas. Bowman can be seen as a Christ figure, sacrificed and resurrected as an omniscient being of light. According to Jung, identification with Christ is a personal development process of the psyche, and if followed by the majority, it would lead to the second coming of Christ.

Thus, the importance of *2001: A Space Odyssey* lies in its potential to engender this elevation of consciousness. However, we must remember that the role of the learned apes of the UN is to keep humanity in Abraxas's grip through technological and matrix control, preventing it from dreaming, and thus from ascending.

CHAPTER 4
The Shining

> Writer, mystic of skill devoid, priorities in lunar sway,
> In Cold War America, cornered, he plays the barman's way.
> "Wife and children?" "Just a little, let me work, I pray."
> "For television?" "Perhaps! a place in Pantheon's array!"

The Shining, along with *Eyes Wide Shut*, occupies the podium for Kubrick's most cryptic, opaque, and subversive films. At first glance, it appears as a relatively incoherent psychological horror thriller, dealing with the descent into madness of a failed alcoholic author.

In truth, Kubrick creates a very personal film where Jack Nicholson embodies the director on screen, and this film resonates as a mea culpa by the director towards his children, his audience, and a reflection on his legacy to humanity and his own karma.

In this section, we will see that *The Shining* is a hermetic confession of the moon landing hoax and the Apollo 11 mission, exposing the pressure and psychological trauma that the deep state inflicted on Kubrick, who was entrusted with the responsibility of the lie and the Western mythology, intended to establish a unipolar world and bide the people's time until the widespread implementation of the global mind control system, which was planned to start in 2001.

Overlook Hotel

The word "overlook" translates to "neglect" or "negligence." The mountain hotel that Jack Nicholson, who represents Kubrick, is tasked with maintaining during the harsh winter symbolizes America that has been neglected by its administrators and which, mired in the Cold War, must maintain its hegemony.

The elements that indicate this are as follows: As in many Stephen King books, the site was built on an Indian burial ground, just like the United States; the various lounges of the Overlook bear the names of American states; The hotel manager, who interviews Jack Nicholson for a job, has the traits and behavior of JFK, who initiated the space race; American flags are scattered all around the hotel, even on the trash cans.

"Image 1" "Image 2" "Image 3"

The Job Interview

"Image 1"

Extract from public JFK's speech 1963 Address to nation

The film begins with a tour of the hotel and its various parts, introducing the responsibilities of the "caretaker" role. The job interview feels like a briefing and a warning about the difficulty of the role, but Jack Nicholson seems excited about this "opportunity," which will allow him to devote time to writing his novel. What could be better for a man with alcohol problems than isolation? No temptations, just peace and free time.

The hotel manager, sporting a toupee, resembles Kennedy in appearance and gestures, and on his desk is an American flag and behind his head, the royal eagle of state power. This is Jack's second job interview for the role, and it becomes somewhat apparent that he was somewhat trapped by the scale of commitment and by a deliberate retention of information when the manager explains what happened to the previous caretaker, Mr. Grady, who, following a nervous breakdown, killed his family before taking his own life. It's a real mess, pardon the expression, that Jack Torrance is offered, and he is forced to accept the role.

Also notable on his desk is the presence of a large red book, which is most likely a reference to Carl Jung's *Red Book*, already mentioned here and to which I dedicate a section in this analysis.

In 1961, Kennedy promised America that it would land on the Moon within ten years. This ambitious announcement of the Apollo program, amid the Cold War and an ideological war for the control of minds or "soft power," represented a financial abyss whose successive failures made the world doubt the competence of the United States.

The Shining takes on full meaning when we understand that Kubrick was recruited/coerced by the American government to take care of a neglected America during the Cold War by its bureaucracy, to achieve an ideological victory by staging and broadcasting on television, thanks to the media machine, the success of the Apollo 11 mission. This was supposed to accommodate everyone involved in this mad race, including the communists, as already suggested by the Russian ambassador in *Dr. Strangelove*.

Just as Jack Torrance is recruited here to take care of the Overlook Hotel during the winter, Stanley Kubrick was recruited by the deep state to take care of America during the Cold War.

Shining and Intuition

The Shining is what you need to deeply understand Kubrick's films, especially this one. The term literally means both "shine" and "gloss" and refers to the world of spirits in the Gold Room, and to the special communication ability some characters in the film possess. This is the case with Jack's son, Danny, and the supporting character Hallorann, an African American funk enthusiast, who recognizes Danny's special ability and explains its workings while warning him to stay away from room 237. We learn in this exchange that the Shining manifests in dreams to convey key information, and in waking life as synchronicities, such as when Hallorann calls Danny by the nickname his parents usually use, Doc.

This "intuition" leads Danny to uncover the history of the Overlook through his visions of the twin girls and the diabolical pact his father signed with the "spirit of the shining people." The Shining induces what we might clinically describe as an epileptic state, which was once sought after by shamans and certain priests whose melancholy and black bile were sources of creative impetus, as described by Aristotle, for communication with gods and divinities or in many rituals sometimes accompanied by wine or other psychotropic substances.

Jung considered intuition one of the essential poles of personality that is developed depending on the individual, acting as a gift that allows for the unconscious or "divine" translation or understanding of sensitive experiences into conscious teachings and enabling the foresight or premonition of future events. Battling the forces of evil can only be done in an intuitive and symbolic manner.

This gloss, or the shiny and invisible layer that covers the paint and adds prestige while hiding and protecting flaws, is elusive, and though one might approach it ambitiously, it is never truly captured; this world is intangible, made of images that generate fear or joy through dreams and hallucinations, much like the lady in the bathroom; it's an illusion comparable to the world beyond the rainbow in *Eyes Wide Shut*, a high principality, a power broth of tribalism and hierarchical relations, possessing almost divine omnipotence through its technical control.

This illusion drives some men to sacrifice their children, just as Jack and Grady do, to secure their place in the pantheon and their pictures in history books.

Wendy, Peter Pan, and Hook

Let's do some casual psychoanalysis around the not-so-random choice of the name of his wife's character, Wendy, played by the quirky Shelley Duvall. In the symbolic study of fairy tales, Wendy is the average little woman who marries a young man (Peter Pan) in hopes that he will one day mature and develop his potential.

The character of Peter Pan, whose name in Greek means totality, represents this unfulfilled potential that risks being lost on the island of lost children, since when one is "everything" at once, one is nothing. Captain Hook represents his ultimate stage of evolution, an adult who has not developed his potential and drowns in resentment and violence, Captain Hook or Hook in English, a pairing reminiscent of Alex and the tramp from *A Clockwork Orange*.

Here, Jack Nicholson embodies this figure of Captain Hook, consumed by his addictions and meager talent, developing strong resentment, which he projects onto his wife and son as his relationship with the Shining, awakened by his alcohol consumption, evolves.

Thus, Kubrick expresses his guilt and judges himself harshly for having been a terrible father, probably neglectful and distant when he was entrusted with his burden, while attempting to explain the causes.

Spirits and Spirituous

"Image 1"

Spirits first manifest in Jack following a fit of anger brought on by his writer's block, which he takes out on his wife Wendy after she accuses him of mistreating their son, Danny.

It's Lloyd, the diabolical-looking bartender in the Gold Room, who reconnects Jack with the world of spirits and hard liquor by serving him whiskey on credit, reawakening his alcoholism and murderous frenzy. Later, Lloyd refuses his payment, indicating that the house takes care of everything. Jack, much like Kubrick, does not truly know who he is working for and feels an attempt at corruption, yet he is paid to do the job, and the rest does not concern him.

Shining is what Jack dreams of as he wishes to join the brilliant guests of the Gold Room, which resembles a 1930s cabaret. The tables topped with luminous crystal balls are reminiscent of those at the Sonata Cafe from *Eyes Wide Shut*, which also triggered Dr.

Harford's confrontation with the invisible elite at the black mass invitation. The protagonist realizes the deception he's a part of during his second visit to the now bustling Gold Room, where he is ignored by all the wealthy and carefree guests despite his conspicuous presence and is warned by the waiter Grady, himself a former caretaker of the hotel who sacrificed his two little girls. The hierarchy of the deep state becomes apparent, and Kubrick is merely an applicant, as the valet and bartender hold authority over him. This scene acts as a reminder of his responsibilities, akin to Zelensky's reception at the NATO summit in July 2023, where he was ignored by the elite in his military outfit and boots, despite doing their dirty work.

The invisible elite is whom Kubrick thought he was joining by making a pact with the devil, only to be treated as an underling, much like Zelensky.

Apollo 11

Let's delve a bit into Kubrick: it's impossible to believe that the numerous obvious clues pointing towards Apollo 11 are coincidental. There are two possible interpretations. Either Kubrick wanted to support existing rumours and play with his audience by making them believe he really filmed the hoaxes. But to what end? It's hard to say, maybe just to showcase his technical mastery? The other possibility is that these rumours were true. In any case, the clues are plentiful.

As with all truths, you'll find analyses everywhere that refute these theories or ridicule them. If it were just *The Shining*, we might doubt it ourselves. But when you relate *The Shining* to the rest of Kubrick's filmography and the themes he raises, there is no doubt. Add to this the mass of evidence documented elsewhere that proves Apollo 11 was a hoax, and it can be asserted without a doubt that this theory is the only truth. Of course, you will have a host of scientists assuring you of the opposite – they have unfortunately overused their argument and lost their credibility, so let's ignore them!

First, there's little Danny, dressed in his Apollo 11 sweater, playing on the floor with his trucks, symbolizing the rocket launch towards room 237, or the 237,000 miles to the Moon, where he will become aware of the horror of his father's deception. In this scene, Danny is the rocket.

"Image 1" "Image 2"

The change from room 217 in the original novel to room 237 in the film has intrigued many. The number 237,000 miles, representing the average Earth-Moon distance, supposedly travelled by Apollo 11 in 23 hours to reach the moon in 1969, might offer a clue as to why this alteration was made. This connection suggests a possible layer of hidden meaning that Kubrick incorporated into the film, potentially alluding to the moon landing, which has been a subject of conspiracy theories, including those suggesting that Kubrick was involved in staging it.

Immediately after this metaphorical "launch" of Danny, or the Apollo 11 rocket, towards room 237, the scene shifts to Wendy trying to activate the strange boiler room, which resembles more a rocket ignition room. As soon as she activates these "reactors," a vivid reaction occurs in Jack, who is asleep at his desk and struggling in a nightmare.

This sequence might symbolize the ignition of the moon mission itself and its profound psychological impact on those allegedly involved in the deception. Kubrick uses the boiler room's activation as a metaphor for starting a powerful and uncontrollable process. Jack's nightmare during this moment can be interpreted as a manifestation of the inner turmoil and moral conflict experienced by someone burdened with such a profound secret.

Through these carefully crafted scenes, Kubrick may be communicating the intense internal conflict between public facade and private truth, reflecting his commentary on the psychological burden of living a dual life—publicly celebrating technological achievement while privately grappling with the ethical implications of deception.

"Image 3"

In room 237, Jack confronts the horror of the illusion of beauty: a young woman taking a bath, portrayed by a Swiss model, far surpassing his own wife in terms of superficial qualities, who then transforms into a decrepit old woman. This scene reinforces the theme of disillusionment, mirroring Kubrick's own perceived deception: a grandiose project turned into torment.

Furthermore, the Indian decorations on the walls of the office, where Jack Nicholson frenetically throws his tennis ball, resemble rockets taking off. This imagery could symbolize the launch of Apollo 11—a pinnacle of technological achievement used to propagate a potentially false narrative, symbolized by the recurring motif of appearances versus reality within the film.

Kubrick's meticulous attention to detail in these scenes may be read as a commentary on the duality of human endeavour: the public spectacle versus the private truth, and the beautiful façade that conceals decay and corruption. The transformation from beauty to decay in room 237 could also reflect Kubrick's disillusionment with the American dream, and by extension, the space race—a beautiful vision marred by underlying moral compromises.

"Image 4" "Image 5"

The third element that explicitly points to the Apollo 11 connection is found when Wendy discovers the extent of her husband's madness and obsession. The phrase "All work and no play makes Jack a dull boy" is repeatedly typed on the writer's tool, his typewriter. The phrasing subtly changes to "A11 work and no play makes Jack a dull boy," with "A11" serving as a potential abbreviation for Apollo 11. Thus, the phrase can be interpreted as: "Apollo 11 work and no play makes Jack a dull boy," suggesting that the intense focus on the Apollo 11 project—or its staged counterpart—has driven Jack to madness.

This clever play on words encapsulates the thematic essence of *The Shining*, weaving the personal with the professional and the psychological with the mythical. It subtly suggests that Jack's mental breakdown is not only a result of his isolation and personal failures but is also tied to the monumental burden of the Apollo mission, whether it be the weight of its secrecy or the moral implications of its alleged deceit. Kubrick uses this repetitive text to signify the mind-numbing, soul-crushing effects of living a lie, an echo of the façade maintained by the Apollo mission.

Kubrick was thus entrusted with a disconcerting mission that he could not refuse, either due to ambition or coercion. Initially appearing as a beautiful young woman, the mission became akin to an aged, decrepit old woman when fully embraced, leading him to neglect his family life, much like a resentful alcoholic might mistreat his loved ones.

Saving an America neglected by its corrupt administrators was certainly no easy task. This allegory, woven into the narrative of *The Shining*, highlights the moral and psychological dilemmas faced by Kubrick—if we subscribe to the interpretation that he was involved in fabricating the Apollo moon landing. The transformation from beauty to decay symbolizes the disintegration of idealistic visions under the weight of reality and moral compromise, mirroring the broader theme of disillusionment in America during the Cold War.

Monarch Project

Just as in *A Clockwork Orange*, where there is a clear reference to the CIA's MK-Ultra program named Monarch, referring to the Monarch butterfly that emerges from the cocoon of trauma endured during programming—consisting of psychological and physical torture of the subject, as experienced by Alex in the film.

In this scene, one can identify all the essential elements of the mind control project: the Monarch poster, the presence of a telephone booth, a radio, and a water cooler (elements that also appear in the bizarre scene with the bear and the aristocrat). These are recurring elements in Kubrick's work, notably in *Eyes Wide Shut*, and he seems to want to establish a causal link between mental programming, radio, telephone, and beverages.

Looking back, one might venture to ask if the twin girls were not a symbolic representation of the demolition project of the Twin Towers on 9/11/2001, which was actually the second major step long planned in the rollout of the global mind control project: to create a terrorist threat through the controlled demolition of the Twin Towers, the objective being to inflict the necessary terror to make people accept the organizational structures of mass surveillance, with the first test step of the storytelling being the success of the Apollo 11 project.

Junk Food and Mind Control

Jack experiences a significant setback when Wendy strikes him with a bat and locks him in the pantry. Dazed, he wakes up on sacks of flour, and it is noticeable that, unconsciously, he has taken the time to snack on Oreos and other packaged or canned goods clearly positioned to his right. Following this, he struggles to his feet and is visited by Grady, the previous caretaker, who reminds him of his duties.

"Image 1"

In the scene where Jack gets up, there are several noteworthy details that can be interpreted within the broader context of the film's themes of control and societal systems:

Heinz Kosher Pickles: The prominently placed can of Heinz kosher pickles could be interpreted in various ways. One interpretation might be that it subtly refers to historical and complex relationships between different groups, such as Germans and Jews, particularly given the historical context of Heinz and its German origins. This might hint at broader themes of reconciliation or hidden collaborations within the film's narrative about societal control and historical memory.

SYSCO Box: The appearance of a box with the SYSCO logo, a major global food distributor that supplies food to company cafeterias, prisons, hospitals, and subcontractors like Sodexo or Aramark, underscores the theme of widespread, systematic control through food supply. SYSCO, being a major player in the food industry, symbolizes the commodification and corporatization of food, which is a crucial element in controlling populations (e.g., in institutions like prisons and hospitals where individuals have little choice over their diet).

SERCO Box: The box labelled "SERCO" introduces another layer of institutional control. SERCO is known for managing diverse public services, including hospitals, prisons, and military bases. The inclusion of this box may suggest the pervasive reach of corporate entities in public sectors, highlighting the intertwined nature of private companies and public services. This connection raises questions about the influence and motivations of such corporations in public life and how they might also be involved in broader control mechanisms within society.

These details in the pantry scene enrich the narrative by suggesting that control and manipulation extend beyond psychological tactics and supernatural elements in the hotel.

"Image 2"

This scene appears to suggest that one of the key elements of mind control lies within the food industry; indeed, when Jack consumes food, he becomes more suggestible to the influences of the characters from The Shining, much like when he consumes alcohol, as demonstrated by his interaction with Grady, who ultimately frees him.

The presence of food items from major distributors like SYSCO and SERCO in the pantry can be interpreted as a metaphor for the mass control exerted through the food supply chain. The implication is that the food industry, by controlling what people eat, can also influence their behaviour and mental states—potentially making them more amenable to other forms of manipulation, and possibly increase their magnetism vulnerability to radio frequencies.

The other key element of mind control as presented by Kubrick is the technology of broadcasting: television, radio, telecom, and all technologies that enable the transmission of waves. These technologies are often depicted as mediums through which control is exerted over the masses. By broadcasting specific messages and controlling the flow of information, these technologies can shape perceptions, influence emotions, and even manipulate behaviours.

In Kubrick's works, technology and control often intersect in ways that highlight their potential for abuse in the hands of powerful entities. In *The Shining*, just as food and alcohol serve as physical mediums influencing Jack's mental state, broadcasting technologies represent a broader, more pervasive method of societal control.

Radios and the SERCO Hint

"Image 1" "Image 2"

The company named SERCO, headquartered in Hook, UK, is a contractor for various public services. At the time of *The Shining*'s release, SERCO was known as RCA Services Limited and primarily specialized in defense technologies, surveillance systems, and radio communications as part of the Radio Corporation of America.

The name SERCO (Services Company) was adopted by the organization in 1987 when it was listed on the London Stock Exchange. It's intriguing to consider whether Kubrick might have been aware of this forthcoming change, or if the organization was already informally referred to by this name. Could this be the reason why Kubrick gives us a close-up of Mr. Torrance disassembling a radio to remove its integrated circuits?

A quick look at their website reveals the sectors in which SERCO operates: from managing satellite contracts for the U.S. military to handling infrastructure for transportation, certain tunnels, ports, airports, hospitals, and some judicial services. Originally focused on telecommunications, SERCO has expanded its portfolio to include activities that are strategic and essential, gradually becoming a private actor with substantial power. It controls information, technology, and operations not just in the countries of the 5-Eyes alliance but also in many European Union countries and Hong Kong. These sectors of activity are also addressed in *A Clockwork Orange*.

Functioning like a private administrative militia, this publicly traded private organization conquers markets by utilizing all available resources to do so and to protect its interests. It has been involved in numerous scandals and plays a significant role in the logistics of human migrations—an organization too opaque to prove direct wrongdoing and too big to fail. The blend of civilian and military activities blurs the lines that once separated these areas, placing military resources at the service of public services managed by a private organization. The existence of such an organization poses a threat to the most basic freedoms and subjects us to their goodwill.

Kubrick's focus on the radio in the film could symbolize the deeper connections and influence that corporations like SERCO have over both public and private sectors, reflecting a pervasive, almost imperceptible form of control that transcends traditional boundaries between government and private enterprise. This portrayal aligns with Kubrick's thematic exploration of power and control, suggesting a world where the distinction between the watchers and the watched becomes increasingly blurred.

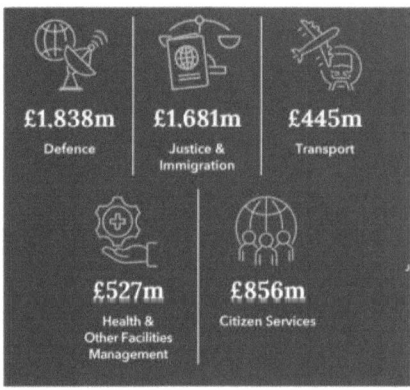

SERCO Activities, extract from annual financial statements 2022 (public)

Television

The new mysticism is broadcast on television, which its viewers receive as gospel truth, without the need to go to church on Sundays.

One accesses science, necessary knowledge, and state mythology from their living room, accumulating knowledge that a remote community in Oregon might not need, unlike practical techniques such as growing carrots or starting a fire.

In this context, a 10-year-old child can vehemently claim to know everything about cannibalism. Similarly, an adult might claim to know in detail the technical feats and technological advances that allowed Americans, in 1969, after many failures and financial losses, to finally plant a flag on the Moon, bring back quantities of lunar rocks now lost, take a buggy ride with little golf carts, and return safely, in a naval capsule that splashed down off the coast of Hawaii, all in less than 10 days.

And so, below we see Danny being reassuring about the project, while Kubrick (Jack Torrance) seems much more skeptical about his ability to make the whole world swallow such a big pill. Despite the powerful medium of television and its certain technical capabilities, it is a risky enterprise in which he might get hurt.

But if they show it on television, it must be true, right?

"Image 1"

"Image 2"

The Cold War

As winter asserts its presence over the Overlook Hotel, covered by a snowstorm, the viewer witnesses the symbolic unfolding of the Cold War, opposing the Western bloc to the Communist bloc. The invisible elites at the top presumably lie together and captivate the minds of the youth, with communism represented by the teddy bears. This is yet another depiction of the deep state theme, and the origin of this global conspiracy of mind control. It is well known that people referred to the Russian bear. Otherwise, what would be the point of this strange scene suggesting a sexual encounter between a man dressed as a bear and an aristocrat, which starkly contrasts with the tone of the film?

In the novel, Horace Derwent, who resembles an English aristocrat, is the former owner of the Overlook, a powerful mafia and casino boss who notably owns United Airlines. The character in the bear costume is a servile figure whom Horace enjoys inviting for sexual favors, creating a sort of sadomasochistic relationship.

If you pay attention to the scene below, you can see the freshwater dispenser, just like in the scene with the Monarch twins.

"Image 1"

"Image 2"

"Image 3"

One of the last arguments that the few remaining proponents of the official Apollo 11 theory, akin to religious zealots, will still advance is the following: if the race to the moon was a hoax, the scientific community of a communist Russia would have debunked it.

Alas, this argument does not hold, as it seems that the communist and American elites, as Kubrick exposes here, were two sides of the same coin. Their common objective was the establishment of a global control system, based on a mythology that included the space conquest by North America as the first step towards progress in a multi-planetary civilization, or rather, a total global mind control technocracy. This deep state, which includes scientific communities, the banking system, and the military-industrial complex, is all stateless, progressing against the people methodically, step by step. The communist infiltration of the United States was already at an advanced stage, as Kubrick had shown in *Dr. Strangelove* made in 1964, where we see the collusion of former Nazis, Russia, and America at its peak, notably through the British.

To create a global unipolar world, which was more or less the case from the 1980s to the 2000s thanks to the success of Kubrick's hoax, a winner had to be designated. This is what Kubrick offered to the Western elite, for a time at least.

This theory is demonstrated daily by facts that show the complete abandonment of Western peoples by their corrupt communist elites who seem to have switched sides at the time of the Soviet bloc's dissolution, leading us steadily towards a new global bloodbath. This ultimate sacrifice, the necessary shock for the acceptance and advent of a world government and a new form of humanity, enhanced by machines and remotely controlled by military technologies, the masses have yet to comprehend, being too occupied with making ends meet and saving what can still be saved, illusionary.

This planned bloodbath, already well underway in Ukraine and Israel, will see the creation of a global hyperclass and the leveling down of the upper middle classes, resulting in a world composed of elites and slaves feeding the fertile belly of Moloch, reminiscent of Fritz Lang's *Metropolis*.

"Image 4"

What does the NASA actually do?

If the preceding is true, one is entitled to wonder what NASA might be doing if not just engaging in communication. While Elon Musk is now striving to land rockets with an eye toward profitability and reusability, he was not well-received when he entered the scene in 2002, in what seemed to be a toxic and unproductive administration. In a speech that has now disappeared from the internet, criticisms rained down, reminiscent of his more recent arrival at the helm of Twitter. Following the media victory of 1969, the pinnacle of the empire of lies, it seems NASA rested on its laurels, no longer sending anyone to the Moon and making no notable advances since then. More recently, NASA raised funds by selling cheap watches under the unregistered NASA brand.

Or, without giving them too much credit, their purpose might lie elsewhere, intertwined with intelligence services and new military technologies whose funding is covered by marketing departments, special effects, and communication strategies that conceal their true end. Incidentally, Australia has a space program as well.

In conclusion here, I will simply repeat the question. So, what exactly does NASA do?

The Labyrinth

"Image 1"

As viewers of Kubrick's films, we experience a feeling similar to that of Jack Torrance, whose internal state is suggested in the scene where he overlooks and observes the model of the maze, searching for the right path only to eventually get lost and die of cold. At this stage of the analysis, we do not have all the elements to fully understand the entirety of the globalist project. Where is the exit? If you wish, you can leave here, you still have a chance. There will be no turning back after the analysis of *Eyes Wide Shut*.

Like exploring a labyrinth, the process of individuation involves confronting difficulties in the search for the centre of the soul, a necessary journey towards consciousness, to finally emerge from the labyrinth stronger. In this journey, one will have faced their fears and discovered the spirit of depths. Each person, at the centre of their personal labyrinth, will find either a symbol or death.

Jung, The Red Book, and the Bloodbath

I propose here an opening that belongs to the realm of intuitive reasoning: I am convinced that Kubrick had knowledge of C.G. Jung's manuscript. Indeed, as already explained, there are numerous references to Jung, the psychoanalyst and great explorer of the human soul, who posthumously published the following mystical book: *The Red Book*. This manuscript, which some describe as "Christian Kabbalism" and written by Jung following the medieval method of the alchemists, was completed in 1930 but was only published publicly under the direction of his relatives in 2012. Some sources suggest that Jung was a hidden descendant of Goethe, one of the most famous Bavarian Illuminati, these potential successors of the Templar order fuelling many conspiracy theories.

On the desk of the hotel director, we see a large red book titled "Red Book," and it seems that the elevator scene also references a passage from the book, which I quote here, an excerpt from *The Red Book - Liber Primus* - Chapter Solution:

"You wanted this war. This is good. For if you had not wanted it, the evil of this war would be insignificant. But with your will, you have made this evil important. If you fail in making this war the greatest of evils, you will never learn to overcome the act of violence and the struggle with what is outside of you. Therefore, it is good that you wholeheartedly want this evil which is the greatest of all. You are Christians, you chase after heroes and await redeemers who must take suffering upon themselves for you and spare you the Golgotha. Thus, you build a mountain of calvaries that covers all of Europe. If you succeed in making this war a dreadful evil and in throwing countless victims into this abyss, it is good, for it will make each of you ready to sacrifice yourself. For like me, you approach the fulfillment of the mystery of Christ. You already feel the iron fist of inflexibility on your neck. This is the beginning of the path. When blood, fire, and cries of distress fill this world, you will recognize yourselves in your actions: drink your fill of the bloody horrors of war, satisfy your hunger for killing and destruction, then your eyes will open, and you will see that it is you who bear such fruits. [...] But at the core, you are horrified by yourselves, which is why you prefer to run towards everything else rather than towards yourself. I have seen the mountain of sacrifice, and blood flowed profusely from all sides. When I saw what pride and strength filled men, what beauty shone in the eyes of women when the great war broke out, I knew that humanity was on the path of self-sacrifice. The spirit of the depths has seized humanity and imposes self-sacrifice on it. Do not seek responsibility here or there. The spirit of the depths has taken hold of the destiny of men, just as it has taken hold of my destiny. It leads men to the mystery through this flood of blood. In the mystery, man becomes himself the two principles, he becomes lion and serpent."

This passage reflects the deep, transformative journey that Kubrick portrays in his films, a journey that involves confronting one's darkest aspects and ultimately transcending them. It is a path filled with suffering and sacrifice but also with the potential for profound personal and collective transformation. Kubrick, much like Jung, delves into the depths of the human psyche, exploring themes of conflict, sacrifice, and the quest for meaning in a seemingly chaotic world.

"Image 1"

"Image 2"

In Kubrick's portrayal, the inevitable bloodbath anticipated by Danny as he turns a corner, symbolizing humanity's elevation and the identification of man with the Christ ideal through self-sacrifice, is vividly depicted.

Is *The Red Book* by C.G. Jung a protective text that could elevate humanity back to the soul and self-sacrifice, much like the Bible has done over the past 2000 years? This might be what Kubrick is suggesting. In this regard, I highly recommend reading *The Red Book*, which possesses genuine magical power, to avoid the coming bloodbath. Also, read and understand the hidden message in Jack Nicholson's hand, which I have attempted to elucidate here.

In this narrative, Jack Nicholson embodies the figure of the Antichrist, striving to shine outwardly while being empty inside, pushing him to neglect and even sacrifice his own offspring. The final image of the film shows Jack Nicholson at the head of the Shining pantheon, protecting the brilliant and unsettling beings of the Gold Room, who pull his arm to prevent him from revealing the message hidden in his right hand. His posture resembles that of Baphomet as depicted by Eliphas Levi, a figure idolized by the Order of the Temple. This is another reference to the Order of the Temple, or what some call the Illuminati.

Kubrick, clearly initiated into the secrets and of immense ambition and pride in the 1970s, found himself in the ungrateful role of Baphomet from his perspective, for which he had to sacrifice his family relationships. He could only recount his experience hermetically, due to the threats he faced, 20 years later in *The Shining*.

The same network likely persuaded Kubrick's daughter, Vivian, who had vocally protested on social media against the handling of the COVID-19 pandemic, vaccines, "wokism," and gender change, to abandon her fight. She seems to have been called to order, as she very suddenly stopped her fervent activism, which would have "had the worst consequences for her and her family" if she had continued.

Let's look at some evidence of this through her Twitter articles and one of her last statements from 2021, where she mentions the Age of Aquarius. According to Jung in *Aion*, this is a dark age that will acknowledge the existence of the devil and witness the coming of the Antichrist.

Kubrick's films and the symbolic references within them, such as the labyrinth, the role of Jack Nicholson, and the allusions to Jungian and Gnostic themes, suggest a complex narrative of human struggle, self-sacrifice, and the search for higher consciousness. *The Red Book* by Jung offers a mystical and psychological roadmap that could guide humanity through its darkest times towards enlightenment and self-realization, avoiding the violent fate that seems to loom on the horizon. The suppression of dissenting voices, like Vivian Kubrick's, highlights the ongoing struggle against forces that seek to maintain control over the collective psyche. Understanding these layers of symbolism and the deeper messages within Kubrick's work might provide insight and hope in navigating these challenging times.

"Image 1"

Baphomet from Eliphas Levi, Dogme et rituel de la haute magie, tome 2, Paris, Germer Baillière, 1861 (public domain)

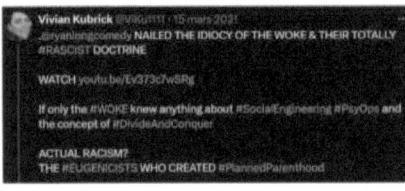
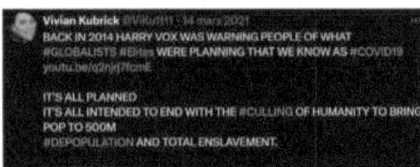

Hey Everyone 😊 👍

First, I want to let you know, I'll be spending less time on Social Media, so won't be posting as much.

It will be hard to do 😔 because it's really gratifying and fun communicating with you all 😊 AND I definitely know how incredibly important it is to exchange information and discuss ideas.

But, what I'm thinking is: we all need to create new lives for ourselves in this BRAVE NEW "NORMAL" and figure out other approaches to bringing about the change we want to see in the world.

I don't think I'm alone here, but I've also got to break a lot of crazy habits I've formed over these last totally insane 11 months! I want to groove in a whole new routine for myself. I think you know what I'm talking about here, right? 😂 😆 !!

Please tell me I'm not the only one who let things slip and allowed some truly whacky and obsessive behaviors to take hold during 2020!!!

It's been rough, hasn't it?? Well. It's time to dust ourselves off and get back in the saddle! 😊 👍

Let's swap out all the truly upsetting crap in our heads (for me that would be Bill Gates, Covid1984 Klaus Schwab, Agenda 2030, Frankenstein Vaccines & Biden) and instead GET PROACTIVE & POSITIVE! I'll be turning my attention to creating healthy new habits like, exercise, yoga, meditation, and learning new things. I'm going to clean up and reorganize my spaces and make plans!

If you're a good deal more sensible than me, you already did this months ago! 😊

Anyway!

All the amazing and creative ideas we will definitely start having when we focus on positive things, will be easier to manifest if we at the same time, strengthen ourselves by adding healthy & sane behaviors to our daily routines. Right? YES!!!!

Okay, I'm not great at disciplining myself either, but this ability can be strengthened, especially because the necessity level is getting really high for all of us, is it not? YES!!!

I'm going to use the knowledge I gathered during 2020 to inform me about the work I want to do and the changes I want to see in the world, certainly that's going to be part of my new routine.

And definitely, I will be spending time protecting my rights - I hope you'll all add this vital activism to your weekly routine, because we're pretty screwed if we lose all our rights! Right? YES!!!!!

I'll be making a list of the rights I want to protect, putting them in order of the most under attack. Then, I'm going to research the laws that currently protect these rights. Then I'll research who I need to speak to locally, as that's where I have the greatest chance to secure my rights.

I reckon in the USA we might all start with our local Sheriff, as he/she is the assigned protector of Constitutional Law.

So! My friends and Unknown friends!

I pray for all of us that we each receive the invaluable assistance of every higher, GOOD being, Angelic, light workers, healers, from every dimension in this universe, and I ask them to stand beside us during this very difficult time of transformation! THE AGE OF AQUARIUS!

I pray these higher beings and God's Angels give us the strength to pour into the world a constant flow of loving kindness and supportive energy – because, we'll need it!

That constant flow of BEAUTIFUL ALTRUISTIC ENERGY will spiritually sustain us WHILE WE FULFILL OUR OWN AND GROUP PURPOSE!

LET ME GIVE THAT A GALACTIC SIZE *AMEN*!!!

😊 PEACE OUT!

With all my love,

(And 🐻 here's a big cyber bear hug!)

Vivian xxxxxxxxx

CHAPTER 5
Eyes Wide Shut

Mocked by his wife who desires military lover,
Naive doctor gets initiated by Manhattan and Ziegler
Into High Kabbalah, where Israel kings and tribes' hover
In pagan orgies and blood rites: there's no turning over.

This film, released on July 16, 1999, exactly 30 years after the launch of the Apollo 11 mission, merits an entire book for its analysis. While some readers may already be familiar with many hidden secrets in Kubrick's other films, the analysis I present here is unique and justifies a complete rereading of Kubrick's filmography. Without my personal and professional experiences confronting key actors in the network, which I will detail in Volume 3, I could not have deciphered this film. We will need to apply an intuitive exploration method, like *The Shining*, in searching for subliminal messages.

Eyes Wide Shut, despite seeming simplistic and even monotonous, is rich in detail, with an extraordinary preparation spanning over a decade, demonstrating Kubrick's absolute mastery. The film took two long years to make and was released in theatres accompanied by, or perhaps causing, Kubrick's death. Notably, the producers cut more than 20 minutes from the film, and Kubrick showed many signs of paranoia as the film neared completion. It is highly probable that this film caused significant turmoil in high circles, leading to Kubrick's elimination.

On the surface, *Eyes Wide Shut* appears as an analysis of the modern couple and the narcissistic and self-centred Western psyche, framed by an initiation journey over one night leading to individual and collective transformation of the couple, at the expense of their progeny. The couple is blinded by sexual concerns, which seem trivial compared to the future of their little girl and their descendants, for whom they never seem concerned. For a first reading, I recommend Tim Kreider's excellent analysis. To summarize it in one sentence, the film presents the initiation of a couple into the global satanic paedophile elite network.

This already dense reading makes *Eyes Wide Shut* difficult to expose. We will see here that the subject, through numerous links to Kubrick's previous films, far exceeds fiction. It details the hierarchical organization of the deep state, its actors, its functioning, its places of worship, its rites, and the technologies and innovations contributing to the satanic control of divinity and the creation of events allowing the control of global mysticism.

To understand it, we must indeed keep in mind the analyses of previous films: *2001: A Space Odyssey* and the theme of the fusion between man and machine and magnetism mixed with artificial intelligence; *A Clockwork Orange*, mental programming and social engineering; *The Shining*, the secret society of the Gold Room and their control of modern mythology, notably through television and the creation of events like Apollo 11 and September 11, 2001.

Tom Cruise and Nicole Kidman

Actor choices in Kubrick's films are never random. Tom Cruise and Nicole Kidman both have close ties to psychiatry, coming from two seemingly antagonistic schools.

Tom Cruise is a well-known member of Scientology, which Vivian Kubrick was also part of. Cruise has used his notoriety to speak out against psychiatric treatments and antipsychotic drugs. Scientology itself faced heavy attacks following its stance against psychiatry and drugs, relegated to the rank of a cult, and forcing its founder, Hubbard, to embark on the private navy project Sea Org to avoid authorities, mainly due to their attack on traditional psychiatry which supposedly favours alternative treatments resembling psychoanalysis. Detractors of Scientology claim it is a satanic organization inspired by Aleister Crowley, but we will not delve too deeply here as it is difficult to form an opinion on such an opaque religious organization.

However, Kubrick presents Tom Cruise's character as a useful idiot of the system, and he was very displeased with his daughter Vivian's involvement with this organization in later days.

"Image 1"

Ying-Yang

Nicole Kidman, still married to Tom Cruise during the filming of *Eyes Wide Shut*, is an Australian actress from one of the world's largest landowning and cattle-producing families. She is the granddaughter of Sidney Kidman, nicknamed the Cattle King.

Her father, Anthony Kidman, was one of Australia's most renowned child psychiatrists, who died under strange circumstances while fleeing to Singapore after Fiona Barnett, author of *Eyes Wide Open*, accused him of numerous rapes and satanic rituals on children in a NSW Royal Commission. We are preparing a French translation of her book, which will be available very soon, as it is a crucial link in exposing the global occult power, the involvement of psychiatric services, CIA and Australia.

This background information on Kidman is highly relevant in understanding *Eyes Wide Shut*. The film delves into the shadowy world of elite power structures, secret societies, and their sinister rituals. The choice of Kidman, given her family's connections and her father's controversial history, adds an extra layer of depth and authenticity to the film's exploration of these dark themes.

Fiona Barnett
Eyes Wide Open

Drawing from Fiona Barnett for her Book Eyes Wide Open, free of rights

We have here a peculiar couple, intertwined since childhood with the themes dear to Stanley Kubrick, prompting questions about their roles within the oligarchy and who was guiding them. Was Kidman tasked with influencing Scientology, or was Scientology attempting to infiltrate the cabal deeply through Tom Cruise? Was this a media couple whose union aimed to create a balance between the masculine (psychoanalysis) and feminine (chemical treatments) poles? Or did Kidman's union with Scientology serve to better protect the satanic practices of Anthony Kidman, as accused by Fiona Barnett, thereby making Tom Cruise the deep state's useful idiot? Are Scientology and psychiatry two satanic poles vying for global governance? In Volume 3, we will delve further into Australia's international psychiatric system, its connections with the CIA and the global deep state, and the significant role Scientology plays in the Australian religious scene, particularly with their acquisition of the Australian acoustic research laboratory in Chatswood.

On screen, Tom Cruise and Nicole Kidman play Dr. Harford and his wife Alice, a general practitioner and an art gallery manager who doesn't seem overly concerned about financial failure; they live a comfortable life in a nice three-room apartment in the gay neighborhood of Greenwich Village, New York, with their young daughter Helena. Their life seems well-ordered, and as they prepare for Christmas, the trees shine, and the city glows under the snow.

The opening depicts the routine daily life of a couple who no longer engage in intimacy, with attentions that are anything but reptilian. Tom Cruise appears bland and unexciting to Nicole Kidman despite his status or "persona," and his inflated persona is evident as he flashes his checkbook and doctor card. Jungian concepts abound in *Eyes Wide Shut*: persona, shadow confrontation, anima/animus, thinking/feeling, etc.

The couple prepares for the annual reception of patient Ziegler, a wealthy and powerful man about whom little is known, who hosts an annual lavish reception for the New York elite.

To analyze this film calmly, we first need to understand its structure and form. The film takes place over a short period, but much happens within it. Kubrick stages the psychological transformation resulting from initiation into the secret society that governs the world and the collective unconscious.

The film centers on Dr. Harford's psychological awakening, who, through gradual steps, experiences a fortuitous initiatory call, like a desire to bring to consciousness the buried and dark aspects of his own subconscious, triggered by drug use and his wife's confession of an infidelity fantasy. We follow him on a dreamlike journey through New York.

Through this initiation, the characters confront their shadows and discover the relationship between the spirit of the depths and the spirit of the times, or in other words, between the personal unconscious and the collective unconscious. They find that, being unsatisfied, they seek elsewhere what they do not have at home, which is a form of human tragedy. There is no happy ending here.

The film presents symmetry around the orgy scene and explores visual and auditory opposites. The initiation begins at Ziegler's reception and continues with the humiliating "fantasy" confession from his wife that knocks him off his pedestal. Mirrors are everywhere: the secretly enamored patient's daughter, whose future husband is his spitting image; the prostitutes Domino and Sally; Domino and Alice; and Domino and Helena.

Tom Cruise and the viewer wander through New York's streets, naive, honest, and passive in their interactions because awareness is an internal phenomenon. This leads to the orgy and near-exposure, the knowledge of the shadows, and obtaining a rank in the elite in exchange for their souls and that of their little girl, ultimately transformed and held.

In this mirrored presentation, we explore what lies on the other side of the mirror or what is found where the rainbow ends for overly curious gentlemen. It is an alchemical attempt dealing with transformation, seeking to reconcile opposites through Dr. Harford and his wife, Dr. Harford and Nick Nightingale, homosexuality and heterosexuality, material and spiritual, animal desire and family love, prostitution and virginity, good and evil.

Consider the main film poster: a kiss between Kidman and Cruise reflected in a mirror, forming a single face with only Nicole Kidman's eye open, perfectly summarizing the film's theme of the union of masculine and feminine opposites. Ultimately, we see that Nicole Kidman is the couple's lookout, as Tom Cruise lacks what it takes, perpetuating the problem across time and space.

Like *2001: A Space Odyssey*, *Eyes Wide Shut* offers multiple readings: Jungian in its concepts, Masonic in the presentation of satanic rituals, esoteric and scientific in its hidden and occult message. Let us remember that Kubrick was always abreast of the latest scientific and technological advancements, which he was not permitted to speak about openly.

Cinematic Bridges

The Shining

The connection between the reception in *Eyes Wide Shut* and the Gold Room in *The Shining* is particularly striking. Both settings serve as grand, opulent spaces where the elite gather, creating an atmosphere of exclusivity and power. Nightingale, much like Lloyd the bartender, acts as a guide into this hidden world. Lloyd introduces Jack to the supernatural elements lurking within the

Overlook Hotel, while Nightingale guides Dr. Harford into the secret society's ritualistic and decadent world.

"Image 1"

"Image 2"

"Image 3"

The music in *Eyes Wide Shut*, particularly during the orgy scene, mirrors the music in the Gold Room scenes from *The Shining*. This choice of music creates a seamless auditory link between the two films, suggesting that they share not only thematic elements but also a shared universe. The waltz of homosexuals in *Eyes Wide Shut* echoes the sense of otherworldly revelry present in the Gold Room, reinforcing the idea of an elite class indulging in hidden pleasures and maintaining secret power structures.

"Image 4"

"Image 5"

Similarly, in *Eyes Wide Shut*, the green bathroom in Ziegler's house serves as a pivotal location. During Ziegler's opulent party, Dr. Bill Harford is summoned to a green-tiled bathroom where Ziegler reveals the darker aspects of the elite world. This private space becomes a site of revelation and entrapment, as Harford learns about the dangerous and illicit activities of the secret society. The green bathroom symbolizes the hidden, often sinister, truths lurking beneath the surface of wealth and power.

The green bathroom, in both films, represents a space of vulnerability and exposure. The color green, often associated with envy and decay, underscores the corruption and moral degradation of the characters who enter these rooms. The bathrooms are places where façades are stripped away, revealing the true nature of the individuals and the systems they are part of.

The green bathrooms in both films serve as crucial narrative devices, trapping the protagonists and pushing them further into the labyrinth of their respective stories. In *The Shining*, the bathroom encounter accelerates Jack's descent into madness, while in *Eyes*

Wide Shut, the bathroom conversation with Ziegler pulls Harford deeper into the web of the secret society.

"Image 6"

"Image 7"

"Image 8"

Kubrick's *Eyes Wide Shut* and *The Shining* share striking similarities, particularly in the journeys leading to pivotal locations: Somerton and the Overlook Hotel.

Both journeys symbolize a transition from the familiar to the unknown. They represent a crossing into territories where societal norms and personal safety are stripped away, revealing hidden truths and dangerous secrets. The roads through the woods are physical and metaphorical passages into the characters' subconscious, where they confront their deepest fears and desires.

"Image 9"

"Image 10"

2001: A Space Odyssey

In the billiard room scene of *Eyes Wide Shut*, there is an object in the background, possibly a heater or air conditioner, that distinctly resembles the monolith from *2001: A Space Odyssey*. Its placement is undoubtedly intentional. Another recurring element is the video/audio stack, with the radio clearly on when Mrs. Harford confesses her fantasies, prompting Bill to question himself. At Domino's, Bill has one hand on the radio and the other on the phone, while Alice is holding the phone with one hand and has the television on with the other.

These elements reinforce the theory that magnetism and mind control are exercised through exposure to gases and magnetic substances, as well as the use of radio frequencies. We will explore how the discovery of the CMB (Cosmic Microwave Background) and NASA's research contribute to this. All these elements are likely orchestrated by artificial intelligence through cell towers or 5G towers, in a network where each human being is a transmitting and receiving node, with their vibrations, thoughts, and movements analysed, stored, utilized, and induced by this system.

We made the mistake of thinking 2001: A Space Odyssey was a failed or missed anticipation. Eyes Wide Shut is set in 2001, precisely when the global mind control plan and subjugation by artificial intelligence are about to take shape, starting with 9/11, followed by COVID-19.

"Image 1"

"Image 2"

In the scene at Domino's apartment, as Bill is about to cheat on Alice, he leans on a radio when he receives a call from Alice. She is watching a film on television about a man cheating on his wife, smoking a cigarette, and eating cookies reminiscent of the Oreos Jack devours upon waking from a hematoma in *The Shining*. On Domino's bookshelf, there is an introductory sociology book, and on Alice's dining table, a daily newspaper.

"Image 3"

"Image 4"

A Clockwork Orange

In *Eyes Wide Shut*, there are notable parallels to *A Clockwork Orange*, particularly in the portrayal of female nudity. This nudity suggests that the high-ranking elites, such as Ziegler, are akin to Alex, raised in violence and conditioned to protect the existing power structure. Bill Harford, by the end of the film, appears destined to join their ranks.

The Yale frat boys in *Eyes Wide Shut*, who challenge Dr. Harford's masculinity, are a direct nod to the gang of droogs from *A Clockwork Orange*. Their tone and slang invite a comparison that underscores their role as modern-day counterparts to Alex and his gang. Yale, notably home to the infamous Skull & Bones fraternity, has produced numerous American presidents and leaders, adding layers to this parallel.

"Image 1"

"Image 2"

Listening to the Yale frat boys, one can detect a similarity in their intonation and argot to the droogs. Their language and demeanour reflect a blend of entitlement and aggression, reminiscent of the droogs' distinctive speech and mannerisms in *A Clockwork Orange*. This comparison emphasizes the continuity of certain themes in Kubrick's work, such as youthful rebellion, elitism, and the corrupting influence of power.

"Image 3"

"Image 4"

The Blue, the Red, and the Rainbow

"Image 1"

"Image 2"

The colors of the rainbow represent the electromagnetic spectrum of colors visible to the human eye. *Eyes Wide Shut* immerses us in the extremes of the rainbow, namely blue and red, and delves into the wavelengths we cannot see. Violet and ultraviolet are still visible to the naked eye, and their rare pigments in the natural physical universe make them a symbol associated with royalty and the union of extreme poles. Historically, purple dye could only be naturally obtained from the mucus of the murex, a mollusc found in the region of Tyre, present-day Lebanon. It took 10,000 to 12,000 shells to produce 1.5 grams of purple. Kubrick's use of purple refers to this symbol, as seen with Domino dressed in purple in *Eyes Wide Shut*, or with Bowman in a purple robe in *2001: A Space Odyssey*, in the antechamber following the transmutation of poles.

There exists a world of electromagnetic frequencies that we do not see. What was once called ether by alchemists, this element connecting all things, has since 1965 been integrated into the Big Bang cosmological model thanks to the accidental discovery of the Cosmic Microwave Background (CMB) by radio astronomers Arno Penzias and Robert Wilson, which earned them the Nobel Prize in Physics. This discovery likely answers the question: what does NASA do? Starting in 1989, NASA's COBE mission (Explorer 66) reported the first images of the cosmic microwave background, as shown in the image below. On June 30, 2021, the WMAP satellite was launched to map the cosmic microwave background. Was this solely for mapping purpose?

Through his use of colour palettes from blue to red, Kubrick attempts to convey cosmological knowledge related to vibrations, the connection between individual microcosm and macrocosm, between individual psyche and collective unconscious, and what is visible and perceptible versus what is invisible and beyond human sensory perception.

Blue and Red Extremes: These colours signify the visible ends of the electromagnetic spectrum. Kubrick's emphasis on these colours in *Eyes Wide Shut* symbolizes the exploration of both ends of human perception of feelings and beyond.

Violet and Purple: The use of purple in significant scenes symbolizes the union of opposites and higher consciousness. The historical difficulty of obtaining purple dye ties into the rarity and preciousness of this colour, which Kubrick uses to signal moments of transformation and enlightenment.

The discovery of the CMB by Penzias and Wilson brought a new understanding of the universe's origins and structure. NASA's subsequent missions, like COBE and WMAP, aimed to further explore and map this background radiation. Kubrick's films subtly reference these scientific advancements, suggesting a deeper connection between the cosmos and human consciousness.

Kubrick's films use visual and thematic elements to suggest a connection between the microcosm (individual human experience) and the macrocosm (the universe). This connection is central to understanding the deeper layers of his work:

Individual and Collective Unconscious: Kubrick explores how individual psyches are connected to a larger, collective unconscious, much like how individual wavelengths are part of a broader electromagnetic spectrum.

Visible and Invisible Worlds: By highlighting colours at the extremes of human perception, Kubrick draws attention to the existence of frequencies and realities beyond our immediate sensory experience, aligning with alchemical and cosmological concepts of an interconnected universe.

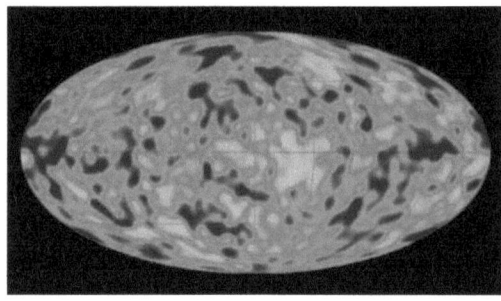

COBE map of fluctuations CMB (FCD), from red to blue, Wikipedia

Kubrick's work indeed suggests an interest in the unseen forces that shape our universe and the potential threats associated with controlling these forces. By delving into themes of vibrations, energy, and frequencies, he invites us to consider the profound implications of understanding and manipulating the invisible aspects of reality.

The idea that the universe is composed of vibrations aligns with the thoughts of Nikola Tesla, who famously stated that to understand the secrets of the universe, one must think in terms of energy, frequency, and vibration. Tesla envisioned a future where the world operates like a single interconnected brain, implying a deep, intrinsic connection between all forms of matter and energy.

The mastery of the CMB, a critical component of the universe's structure, might be seen as a step toward mastering the fundamental aspects of reality itself. This raises profound questions about the nature of control and divinity:

Control of Vibrations: If everything is vibration, controlling these vibrations could theoretically allow for control over matter and energy, essentially giving one power over the physical universe.

Divinity and the CMB: The idea of mastering the CMB touches on the notion of achieving a god-like understanding or control over the cosmos, as the CMB represents the residual radiation from the Big Bang, the very birth of the universe.

In the contemporary context, the official acknowledgment of directed energy weapons adds another layer of complexity to this discussion. These technologies, which manipulate electromagnetic waves, illustrate how advanced our understanding and control of vibrations have become. The dual use of telescopes and satellites for both scientific measurement and potentially other functions suggests that our capabilities may extend beyond mere observation to active manipulation.

Kubrick's films, with their intricate symbolism and exploration of hidden forces, seem to foreshadow these developments. By embedding these themes in his narratives, Kubrick might be educating viewers about the potential and dangers of controlling invisible forces. His work anticipates the convergence of technology, consciousness, and the manipulation of reality, resonating with contemporary advancements in directed energy and electromagnetic manipulation.

Atacama and South Pole telescope 3G, Wikipedia

Masculine – Feminine / Anima - Animus

Jung defines the animus as the masculine part of a woman and the anima as the feminine part of a man, which individuals keep hidden to conform to their gender roles. Jungian therapy involves confronting one's shadow and developing these opposite poles to achieve completeness and unity with oneself and others.

A man who develops his anima becomes more intuitive, capable of feeling and expressing emotions, and develops relational and sociable traits, including tenderness and listening skills. At the beginning of Eyes Wide Shut, Bill Harford appears childlike, likely around 33 years old, an age often associated with spiritual awakening.

A woman who develops her animus gains strength, willpower, the ability to think, speak, judge, and act autonomously in the world. Without integrating her animus, she may appear as a virago confronting men, as Alice seems at the start—capricious and immature.

During the film's initiatory journey, both members of the couple confront their shadows and develop their anima and animus. However, Dr. Harford fails to integrate his anima properly, regressing to a childlike state, while Alice successfully integrates her animus.

Eyes Wide Shut portrays the apex of society—spiritual power and the monopoly of violence—as controlled by men who manage and unite society by manipulating women, their aspirations for power, or their misery. The dynamic between Alice and Bill suggests that control over Dr. Harford is exerted through Alice, who sacrifices her fantasies to protect the collective elite, or the "Shining"—possibly compromised at a young age in this network, which is strongly suggested by her untouchable status, her beauty reminiscent of the naked women in the ceremony, and her words that initiate the journey.

Alice may have been programmed to be the perfect wife for a wealthy man, like Millich's daughter, who is trained in the art of seduction from a young age. This parallels the recent accounts of Anneke Lucas and other survivors of ritual abuse, indicating a pattern of grooming and control.

The Good Doctor

Dr. Harford is a New York physician, and nothing explicitly suggests he is Jewish. There is a seven-branched candelabrum, or menorah, in their home, but it seems likely that his wife, who is responsible for the museum, oversees the decor and the art that adorns their walls.

Harford is depicted as gentle and somewhat naive:

He asks his wife where his wallet is before leaving, even though it's always on his nightstand. He has a gentle demeanour, indicated by his interactions with his daughter, who dressed as a princess wants to watch The Nutcracker and asks for a "watch dog" for Christmas, likely not feeling secure with a father she perceives as lacking charisma.

His repeated small mistakes, dangerous insouciance, identification with his persona, and habit of brandishing money at every opportunity highlight his naivety. His close professional proximity to the "chosen people" suggests his awakening and initiation might be necessary for the security and survival of his "tribe", forcing him into recognizing who holds the actual power over him.

The characters in the film, starting from the Christmas party, are puppets controlled by invisible strings that facilitate the initiation of the gentile into this community. This large-scale didactic experience is orchestrated by an omniscient conductor hidden behind a curtain, with real and irreversible collateral damage and consequences.

Adultery: Thinking - Feeling

The password for the secret party, "Fidelio," is an opera by Beethoven that deals with a wife's fidelity to her husband and the theme of self-sacrifice, reminiscent of Penelope in Homer's Odyssey. The question arises: How much can a woman sacrifice for her husband?

The adultery in Eyes Wide Shut is imagined rather than an actual one. Alice envisions an affair during a waltz with Sandor and fantasizes about a naval officer during one of their first romantic cruises, which calls their entire relationship into question. Dr. Harford is tempted by two prostitutes who invite him to "where the rainbow ends" and has a brief romantic encounter with his brief soul mate, Domino. They are the archetypal desires and phantasms of a man and a woman.

The biblical reference, "What comes out of the mouth proceeds from the heart, and this is what defiles a person. For out of the heart come evil thoughts—murder, adultery, sexual immorality, theft, false witness, slander" (Matthew 15:18-20), underscores the power of thoughts and words: both Alice and Bill's unspoken desires and fantasies introduce tension into their relationship. The unspoken and imagined infidelities reflect deeper issues within their marriage.

The Sermon on the Mount warns that the prohibition of murder includes internal anger, and the prohibition of adultery includes lustful looks. This highlights the importance of internal thoughts and intentions on spiritual life.

Bill Harford's journey is one of existential crisis and self-discovery, questioning his life: Alice's confession of her fantasy with a sailor during their honeymoon throws Bill into turmoil. He questions his entire life, his masculinity, and his previously secure identity as a husband and father.

Bill, a rational doctor accustomed to material comfort and control, is confronted with the irrationality of emotion and animal instinct. His encounters with various temptations and his venture into the secret society force him to confront these aspects of himself. To him, the idea of a woman, married to a wealthy doctor, considering adultery challenges his rational worldview. Alice, who seems to have everything, reveals the complexities of human desire and dissatisfaction.

Throughout the film, Bill transitions from a rational, controlling figure to one who must face the depths of human emotion and irrationality. His journey symbolizes a confrontation with the anima (the feminine part of his psyche), leading to potential self-awareness and growth.

Thus, this spoken thought bore its rotten fruits, giving rise to the reality of that evening. The outcome supposedly does not define their entire relationship, as they emphasize in the final scene, but it alters their state of spiritual awakening and consciousness towards each other. This awakening, however, is induced by a black mass involving a human sacrifice, and for which they symbolically sacrifice their only child. They feel reassured that they have survived and "saved their marriage," as one can observe when the little girl is subtly taken away by strange characters in the toy store. These characters were identifiable in the initial ceremony, and the imagery of tigers recalls the fate of her soul mate, Domino, a young prostitute. A new Kubrickian ouroboros is thus completed.

"Image 1"

"Image 2"

"Image 3"

"Image 4"

This final scene very strangely echoes the ending of Polanski's *Chinatown*, where the big bad wolf, protected by the police, ultimately takes away his daughter, who is also his granddaughter. Polanski's filmography extensively explores themes identical to those in *Eyes Wide Shut*, particularly in *Rosemary's Baby* and *The Ninth Gate*, which certainly merit further exploration and comparison.

"Image 5"

The good doctor, although he seems to have developed his animal instinct and charisma among the prostitutes and homosexuals, is now compromised within the satanic network and subjected to the authority and goodwill of his wife. Indeed, while his relationship with his wife had somewhat evolved, as shown by his newfound ability to listen to her nightmare and offer a comforting shoulder, he failed by revealing the details of his initiation to her. This relegates him to a state of both psychological and physical submission in the final scene, unlike her, who appears to have matured and taken responsibility for the couple. This maturity is evidenced by her behaviour, which has acquired a certain "masculine" maturity compared to her initial juvenile aspect.

For Bill, who betrayed his initiation by revealing it to his wife, it is a lost cause. He relinquishes the power that had been entrusted to him and hands it over to Alice. His animal instinct has faded, reverting to its initial childlike state. His wife has become an instrument of control for this frightening system, as evidenced by her beige trench coat, mirroring the one worn by the bald man recruited by Ziegler to watch over him.

Alice has received orders from the Shining, and she follows them.

Parenthood

As previously touched upon, Eyes Wide Shut questions the condition of parents in a modern materialistic society, governed by occult forces, vices, and narcissistic instincts, where maternal instinct is repressed in favour of fulfilling desires and fantasies. Kubrick seems to take a critical view of this society, suggesting it is either inherently flawed or an inevitable aspect of human nature.

Helena, named after the famous female archetype Helen of Troy, is materially spoiled. Her mother, Alice, shows a lack of passion in caring for her, reflecting a cultural suppression of natural maternal instincts. Helena is discouraged from playing with traditional maternal toys like dolls and strollers, deemed old-fashioned.

Alice educates Helena to become her version of a "good woman," essentially a doll for a wealthy man: the story Alice reads to Helena before bed references satisfying a man sexually. In another scene, Alice helps Helena with her homework by teaching her to count the money in her boyfriend's purse. This indicates that Alice is grooming Helena to prioritize material wealth and male approval over genuine maternal or personal fulfillment.

Domino, a character with maternal instincts and an inverse reflection of Mrs. Harford, is presented as a more grounded, nurturing figure seen through her interactions and the stroller frequently shown, Domino represents the nurturing aspect that Alice suppresses. She appears as a potential soulmate for Bill, wearing the royal violet colour symbolizing a balance in Bill's psyche under a fur coat representing animal instinct. Modest and generous, as indicated by her tidy apartment left for her roommate despite the mess left for her. Her nurturing and simple femininity contrasts with Alice's more complex and materialistic nature. She eventually refuses the money that Bill offers.

On Bill's second visit, Domino is absent, having received a call informing her she is HIV positive. She is replaced by her roommate, whose behaviour mirrors Alice's flirtation with Sandor. Domino's potential as Bill's soulmate is nullified following the black mass, her disappearance symbolized by an HIV diagnosis, potentially administered by a fellow doctor like Dr. Miller, who might prescribe her a costly and harmful HIV treatment.

"Image 1"

"Image 2"

As in *A Clockwork Orange* and *2001: A Space Odyssey*, Kubrick shows us the misery of generational transfer in Western society, governed by vices and materialism, and the vulnerability of parents in the face of an omnipotent network, due to the loss of cultural landmarks and a degenerated supreme spiritual authority.

Masonic Symbols and Rothschild

Throughout *Eyes Wide Shut*, Bill Harford quickly traverses the 33 degrees of the Scottish Rite. The symbolism in certain scenes matches the descriptions of the rites from the "Book of the Ancient and Accepted Scottish Rite." We will take one example to confirm this but will not extend this analysis, which would take considerable time. The main point is to understand that Kubrick presents a Masonic initiation, with Ziegler, whose name means "mason" in Old German, likely being the head of a New York lodge and responsible for Bill's initiation. We will reiterate here that although Kubrick had a deep knowledge of the rites and probably an appreciation for Masonic philosophy, he seems to criticize the Masonic organization, as clearly stated in *Paths of Glory* (1958), for participating in totalitarian power.

Let us analyse the scene below and the description of the 5th degree of the Scottish Rite: "The lodge is draped in green fabric with eight white columns, four on each side at equal distances. An altar draped in black, soaked with tears, is placed in the east. At the foot of the throne in front of the altar is a coffin draped in black, resting on a bier with the jewel and apron of the grand master. Four lights are placed at each of the cardinal points. Marks of blood are present in the northeast."

By comparing this description to the visuals and thematic elements in the movie, we can see how Kubrick incorporates Masonic elements into his storytelling. The lodge setting, the placement of lights, and the symbols of mourning and sacrifice all resonate with the Masonic ritual. This not only underscores the secretive and ritualistic nature of the society depicted in the film but also highlights the broader critique of organizations wielding covert and unchecked power.

"Image 1"

"Image 2"

In *Eyes Wide Shut*, the symbolic elements align closely with the Scottish Rite of Freemasonry. For example, we see green drapery, lights at the cardinal points, a toilet serving as the throne, and a chair draped in black corresponding to the altar. The presence of a corpse above the bathtub in a painting of a nude woman represents the coffin. Each scene follows similar codes and is structured to reference elements of the Scottish Rite.

Later, when Bill realizes he is being followed and hurries his pace, the buildings behind him are numbered 30-31-32-33-34. It is rare to have both even and odd numbers on the same side of a street, yet it is the case here. This signifies that his initiation has surpassed the 33rd degree, his subsequent confrontation with Ziegler confirms this, as Ziegler, appearing flustered, attempts to reassert control over Bill.

Further, the most evident connection to the Rothschild family is the masked ceremony at Somerton. The exterior shots are of Mentmore Towers, an English mansion built in the 19th century for Baron Meyer de Rothschild. The masks used in the film resemble those from a surrealist ball hosted by the Rothschilds in 1972.

"Image 3"

Orgy, Exposure, and Sacrifice

The central scene of *Eyes Wide Shut* involves an extensive visit to Somerton Mansion, a black mass, and the ensuing orgy. Many elements of a traditional mass are subverted: a reversed Hungarian liturgical chant, a priest, an incense burner, and ritualistic forms. Beautiful nude women stand in a circle, seemingly offered to the gods in the sexual orgy that follows.

The choice of Eastern music for the orgy is a South Indian Tamil chant, a Dravidian language like Telugu, which may hold significance. Many Western leaders and technological and spiritual authorities hail from South India: the Theosophical Society chose Krishnamurti as a leader for a new world religion; Ramaswamy, a U.S. presidential candidate, is also Tamil; and the CEOs of major tech companies like Google (Sundar Pichai), IBM (Arvind Krishna), and others are from this region.

An initiation is a rite of passage involving physical or psychological trials that produce trauma or require unforgettable effort to mark the transition from one life cycle to another. The tribal cult in *Eyes Wide Shut* uses terror and public humiliation as initiation methods. The masked characters see the initiate exposed and naked while remaining anonymous behind their masks.

The tribe applies a principle of unity, making someone pay for breaking a rule, either by expiation of the fault or possibly death, depending on the severity. The punishment does not necessarily fall on the one who committed the fault. Thus, faults can be redeemed, not through justice, but by punishing a golem or scapegoat. The most famous example is Jesus Christ, who redeemed the faults of many by dying on the cross, creating the Christian rite. Every Sunday for 2,000 years, instead of self-sacrifice, people expiate their sins in a symbolic human sacrifice, guided by a priest, through prayer and paying for confession, an ancestor of data collection. In a perfect information society, confession becomes obsolete; everything about you is known, so you must behave.

If Bill had not been redeemed by Mandy, he would likely have paid with his life. Many collateral damages result from the Gentile Doctor's initiation, due to the principle of unity, as many rules were broken. Mandy, Nightingale, and Domino all seem to have been punished. The tribe takes no risks and does nothing by its own hand, making dismantling it difficult and requiring intuitive reasoning. Perfect evidence does not exist, and the elite protect each other.

Exposure in this initiation is essential; those contributing to the tribe's life by seniority, status, or blood know all members, while lower-ranking ones only know the new members, hierarchically inferior. Bill's inability to identify any tribe members forces him to be discreet and distrust everyone, showing the magical power of the "Manhattan elite's" ritual. They have all the information on you; you have none on them.

A Thought Experiment in Mind Control

Imagine this ceremony extending beyond Somerton, considering the theory of generalized mind control through magnetism and radio control, orchestrated by artificial intelligence simulating exposure and terrorizing the subject. How would it work?

Harari and the WEF suggest that data centres and AI know us better than we know ourselves; they understand our weaknesses, fears, and deep identities, the symbols and levers to produce specific emotional reactions. In the presence of a conductor for this system, it would be possible to create a personalized, terrifying initiation experience, exposing us before our families, friends, and colleagues, who would have varying levels of control and access to your personal data based on their hierarchical position in the tribe, using the correct levers to exert effective power over you.

This initiation would materialize through our phones, suggesting actions, and our human networks, strategically controlled remotely, often unknowingly, along with the organizational matrix, tools of administrative harassment, to punish or scare us by using the correct levers, likely creating in the target something resembling psychosis or paranoia. Anyone investigating or exposing the system would be pushed to renounce for material reasons; this initiation or punishment would ultimately lead to hospitalization, imprisonment, or, in the worst case, death, depending on your karma and tribal ranking. Remember *A Clockwork Orange* and wonder if Alex's adventure was a significant remote-controlled initiation, ending in a suicide attempt, institutionalization, and promotion for the new initiate.

It seems that what has always a satanic tribal religious ritual, based on rumours and confession, has become a new religion of control through technological means and the omniscience it allows. In its current tribal and satanic form, more sectarian than universal, this new religion exercises terror through an undefined dogma, protecting itself through corruption and threats to its members.

Indeed, the initiated Bill is offered material gifts for his silence: Domino's roommate, the hotel receptionist, Millich's daughter, or a crate of whiskey from Ziegler, many vices the new recruits can indulge in without fearing the tribe's retribution. However, if they try to expose the organization, Helena will be sacrificed. This organization detests good men, rich, childless, and those taking vows of chastity or poverty: they disarm the tribute from their control levers.

Do we want to live in a world governed by this cult?

Medias and the Forgery of Events

Radios, televisions, and newspapers are omnipresent, serving as streams that incessantly shape minds, raise children, suggest actions, and create unconscious symbols that feed a consumerist and vice-driven society.

After his nocturnal adventure, Bill turns to the New York Post, with the headline "Lucky to be Alive," as if placed there to intimidate him and reinforce his sense of powerlessness. And perhaps it was, since we soon learn that the participants in the ceremony were very high-ranking individuals whose names we cannot mention.

The New York Post is one of the famous tabloids owned by News Corp, led by the renowned media mogul Rupert Murdoch. Murdoch, a Presbyterian native of Australia, was a Republican Democrat with communist leanings in his youth. He is a nationalist Scotsman with significant influence, specializing in phone hacking, opposition hacking, and politician bribery. At the helm of a true media and broadcasting empire, including Sky News, Foxtel, The Australian, and others, he is closely associated with the Rothschilds and the Freud family (the psychoanalyst). Through his son-in-law and his business portfolio, he connects to Hollywood, making him one of the major holders of Western mysticism. In Australia, he has spent his life vying for control of the media empire and available brain time with his main competitor, Fairfax.

In the image below, aside from the information about Mandy's death, locked inside her hotel room, we can read details of two actual events that point once again to remote control technologies and the theory of an "event forge" used by the deep state to control mysticism and influence politics. We will later relate this to James Tilly Matthews, his denunciation of the "Air Loom Machine" in 1790, and the resulting psychiatric internment, as well as the Ziegler House, led by Carleton Simon.

The first article from 1996 near New York involves Anthony Norman, a disabled person, likely under medical supervision and treatment, who decided one day to rob a grocery store after, he claimed, "the television suggested it to him." This news parallels Alice's call to Bill, influenced by the television program she was watching.

The second article from 1997 in West Virginia recounts a tragedy where a 29-year-old woman killed her children before committing suicide. This incident mirrors the theme of parental distress and societal pressure present in the film, where characters are manipulated by unseen forces and technologies.

Extract from New York Post Newspaper

> **New York Times**
> https://www.nytimes.com/1996/12/11/nyregion/bank...
>
> ## Bank Robbery Suspect Says He Got Inspiration From TV
> WEB Dec 11, 1996 · **Anthony Norman** has served time for several petty crimes, but when he decided to rob a **bank** on Monday, he says in a statement to the police, he drew his ...

Extract from Google search

The newspapers also mention the case of a mass shooting that took place on a train in Long Island, New York, in 1993. Colin Ferguson began shooting at other passengers with a semi-automatic pistol. Six victims were killed, and nineteen others were injured.

Ferguson's trial was marked by several unusual developments, including his dismissal of his defence attorneys, his insistence on representing himself, and his cross-examination of his victims on the witness stand. He was found guilty in February 1995 of six counts and sentenced to life imprisonment. Moreover, while he admitted to bringing the gun on the train, he claimed that he had fallen asleep, and another man had seized his weapon and started shooting. He also alleged that a mysterious man named Mr. Su had information regarding a conspiracy against him. He had managed to find another individual willing to testify in his favour that the government had implanted a chip in his brain. At the last moment, Ferguson decided not to call this person to the stand.

This individual, Raul Diaz, was a Manhattan parapsychologist who claimed at a press conference on the courthouse steps to have witnessed the insertion of a chip into Ferguson's head before the attack. According to Diaz, it was Mr. Su who suggested what Ferguson would do before pressing the button. "He would have been zapped by a remote-control device," Diaz told reporters outside the courthouse. "He was zapped, just like that, he was remote-controlled to go back and forth in the train, shooting people."

This shooting was subsequently used for political purposes by the wife of one of the victims, a dyslexic Democratic nurse, Carolyn McCarthy, who was elected to Congress campaigning for gun control, abortion rights, and the use of stem cells.

The two cases mentioned above perfectly align with our overall analysis and cannot be a mere coincidence. This is the core subject throughout Kubrick's entire filmography.

Intermission

We have touched upon several themes raised in *Eyes Wide Shut* that reinforce the view that Kubrick was both a keen student of Jung, whom he presents as a key to future global balance, and knowledgeable in alchemy and Freemasonry, particularly the Scottish Rite.

In his film *Paths of Glory* and through the preceding analysis, Kubrick designates Freemasonry as a cornerstone of satanic global governance, not in its message and ritual, which he seems to appreciate, but in its corrupt individuals and leaders. If the message of Freemasonry is that of the free, good, and universal man through a symbolic and historical exploration of spiritual currents, it is evident that it has been hijacked and instrumentalized for control and subjugation.

The message here is: initiate yourself, be good, be free, and do not submit to the unhealthy hierarchy that corrupts you and devours your children.

Eyes Wide Shut is, like *2001: A Space Odyssey*, an initiation into the secrets of the Western world. By cautiously naming the key actors of global domination, Kubrick risks his freedom against the tribe to which he belongs, and he brilliantly accomplishes a great work that everyone, out of jealousy or personal interest, will try to diminish.

What follows will name the individuals responsible.

Ziegler and the Ziegler's House

"Image 1"

"Image 2"

The name "Ziegler" in German denotes a mason, clearly suggesting that we are dealing with a high-ranking Freemason, as highlighted by numerous references to the Scottish Rite throughout the film. The Ziegler in *Eyes Wide Shut* is portrayed as a powerful character, living in luxury far beyond that of the modest Dr. Harford, hosting New York's elite in his home to celebrate Christmas. He is socially adept and always has the right words for the ladies, while his wife seems to tolerate him, likely accustomed to his antics and dependent on him.

From the Christmas ceremony, we can infer that only one character is hierarchically superior to Ziegler: Sandor. Sandor possesses a pronounced charm and self-confidence, demonstrated by his transgressive behaviour with Alice Harford and his ability to access any room in Ziegler's mansion at will, such as when he invites Alice to view private rooms. We will dedicate an analysis point to the character of Sandor. In this scene, while Bill is surrounded by two youthful escort girls, Nicole Kidman is being courted by a Hungarian prince, in what appears to be a coordinated attempt to corrupt our protagonists simultaneously.

It is strongly suggested that Ziegler is the master of ceremonies for the black mass. His movements and gestures conspicuously resemble the reminder scene around the billiards table, where the cue tapped on the ground mimics the rhythm of the ritual sceptre's percussion. Another hypothesis is that the man in the red robe is Sandor, due to his accent. This distinction is relatively minor, as both are closely linked and high-ranking.

Ziegler wields his power unabashedly, removing Bill from his reception in confidence when a prostitute he was with overdoses. He relies on Bill's discretion and perhaps invites him annually for just such emergencies, compromising him while protecting himself.

The exterior of Ziegler's mansion, where the luxurious annual gala is held, is the Consulate General of Poland on Madison Avenue, which points us towards Millich and his Polish accent.

Additionally, there is indeed a real "Ziegler's House" in Manhattan, founded by William Ziegler Senior and Junior, who were the founders of an industrial chemical production trust. Below is a comparison of the interiors of Ziegler's house in *Eyes Wide Shut* and the real Ziegler House.

The spiral staircase, the office, the checkered floor, and the green bathroom are all clues that corroborate the link established by Kubrick between the house in the film and the real Ziegler House.

"Image 1"

Photography by Samuel H. Gottscho (public domain)

"Image 2"

Photography by Samuel H. Gottscho (public domain)

"Image 3"

Photography by Samuel H. Gottscho (public domain)

"Image 4"

Photography by Samuel H. Gottscho (public domain)

Kubrick intentionally sheds light on Ziegler House. But why? Let's delve into the history of the real William Ziegler and this house, which has seen its share of interesting figures. Keep in mind the concept of the "forging of events."

William Ziegler Sr., a Freemason and a Knight Templar, established the first U.S. monopoly in food chemistry, the Royal Baking Company. His adopted son, an orphan, inherited it. Notably, Ziegler Sr. had a dual background in chemistry and telegraphy and was involved in polar exploration, funding several missions to the North Pole under the Ziegler-Baldwin name, including the ship Belgica, which had previously explored the South Pole. It was his son who established Ziegler House in 1926, as seen in the images.

Before Ziegler Jr. established the house, it had notable occupants:

The Havemeyer Family: William F. Havemeyer, a sugar magnate and multiple-term mayor of New York, founded the NYPD, transitioning from the night watch system reminiscent of private security agencies discussed earlier.

Robert B. Roosevelt Jr.: The nephew of U.S. President Theodore Roosevelt and son of Robert Roosevelt, U.S. ambassador to The Hague. Theodore Roosevelt became president after the assassination of President McKinley by Leon Czolgosz.

Dr. Carleton Simon: A New York Jewish psychiatrist, educated in Vienna and Paris, criminologist, and narcotics specialist. He pioneered fingerprint recognition for the American police and invented iris recognition with Isadore Goldstein. He founded and was the general commissioner of the narcotics bureau of the New York police. Simon spent his life arresting drug users and imposing a Hollywood code of conduct through censorship, connecting him to Hollywood's exclusive world. He is known for his clinical study of Leon Czolgosz, who assassinated President McKinley, leading to Theodore Roosevelt's presidency. By 1921, he had collected the identities and fingerprints of over 100,000 narcotics convicts in the U.S. and 27 countries, creating a powerful platform for a control-based organization through blackmail.

Buried in Linden Hill Jewish Cemetery, Carleton Simon stands out as a significant yet under-the-radar deep state actor, whose impeccable biography hides potential nefarious activities aimed at protecting his community's interests rather than the public's, using his charisma as a top-tier psychiatrist. His work often absolved dubious individuals like Emma Goldman and May Johnson. His association with George Francis Train, a powerful transportation entrepreneur involved in the Australian gold rush and the Crédit Mobilier scandal, further underscores it. Train was also a vocal feminist and propagandist.

Thus, Ziegler House in the early 20th century was a hub of schemes, societal control strategies, and social engineering intertwined with the food and chemical industries and polar exploration. Consider that controlling information was simpler then, with the New York Times or New York Post shaping public opinion, and that with the right networks, it was easier to build a saintly aura around well-placed figures like Carleton Simon. This ties into James Tilly Matthews' "Air Loom Machine" concept and its event-forging capabilities.

Today, Michele Simon, a public health lawyer in New York, founded the Eat Drink Politics Institute, promoted in U.S. universities by Professor Marion Nestle. Additionally, I encountered Carleton Simon's descendant, Michelle Simon, in Sydney, Australia. An accountant/psychologist born in Israel, she formerly worked for Coca-Cola, the United Nations, and is now a censor at Uniting

NSW.ACT, Australia's largest Protestant community services organization. Michelle Simon, in her key position, manipulates data and enforces the UN's Agenda 2030 within the organization, disguised under a saintly veneer, causing disastrous community repercussions. I observed her methods up close as a consultant, subtly pushing employees to falsify data, doing nothing herself.

For the first time, these key actors are explicitly and clearly identified. The keystone of this structure, Ferdinand Freudenstein, whose niece Kay Freudenstein, a former News Corp (parent company of the New York Post) IT systems employee, is linked to the Australian casino empire through her husband Hayes and... is Michelle Simon's boss at Uniting NSW.ACT, overseeing IT systems. This organization provides various community services, including child welfare and psychiatric services.

From Ziegler House, the branches of a constellation of deep power players extend strategically to Australia, intertwining communication technologies, chemistry and food industries, law enforcement, community services, and politics. Recall Kubrick's previous films discussing manipulation and programming techniques, magnetism, and artificial intelligence. We are indeed entering troubled waters.

Watchdogs

"Image 1"

The use of "watchdogs" throughout Eyes Wide Shut is a significant symbolic element, representing the surveillance and control exerted by powerful, shadowy figures over the protagonist and the society he navigates. This surveillance is not only physical but also psychological, with various characters and entities ensuring that the established order and illicit activities remain undisturbed.

These guardians are stationed at every club and building, ensuring the smooth operation of a surveillance system that protects the underground economy operating right under our eyes, which are metaphorically wide shut. This economy includes prostitution, paedophilia, trafficking, and ritualistic murders, all lucrative yet prohibited markets that function barely concealed. To see this reality, one must look beyond the Christmas tree and its glittering lights, understanding that all the polish at the top is compromised, including judges, senators, and other deep state officials, constantly watched by these watchdogs of the system, private security organizations, and fraternity members from prestigious universities in their trench coats.

The guards and masked figures at Somerton epitomize the direct surveillance and enforcement of the secret society's rules. They are the visible force maintaining the secrecy and security of the elite's hidden world.

The doorman at the Sonata Cafe symbolizes the gatekeepers of knowledge and entry into exclusive spaces, representing the barriers to uncovering hidden truths and the layers of protection around illicit activities.

The frat boys and the men who follow Dr. Harford signify the pervasive reach of the surveillance network, extending into public and private spaces, ensuring constant monitoring and intimidation.

Millich's Rainbow Fashion shop serves as a central hub for these watchdogs, tying together the various elements of surveillance and control within the narrative. The shop's name itself, with its reference to the rainbow, alludes to the spectrum of visibility and hidden realities within the film.

"Image 1"

"Image 2"

"Image 3"

"Image 4"

"Image 5"

Miller and Millich: Locksmiths and Security

Let's examine the elements that connect Miller and Millich to security services. Mr. Miller is already mentioned in 2001: A Space Odyssey as the head of security on the orbital station who meets Floyd, the UN scientist. Everything in the meticulously crafted Manhattan set created by Kubrick and his team points to Miller: we are on Miller St, beer advertisements display "Miller's Time" - the owner of the costume shop "Rainbow Fashion" is named Millich, the Polish version of Miller. In the street, we also see another clue with the shop named "A Hint of Lace," a play on words suggesting

It seems that Kubrick wants us to understand that the streets of New York are controlled and directed by this villainous character, confident and dominant, with a Polish accent, who is present everywhere around our wealthy Dr. Bill. This same Mr. Miller, to whom our Dr. Floyd reports, suggests a hierarchy or an equal footing.

One might wonder what the point of all this is, considering that he is a fictional character, and maybe it's just a coincidence. But as you now understand, there are no coincidences in Kubrick's work, only clues that appeal to your intuition and connections to the real world that reveal hidden truths, exposing the deep power structures.

Let's return to the character of Millich and the symbols associated with him. If Millich is a cautious character, he is not difficult to buy off. Many elements associate Millich with security symbols, such as the always-closed gates, access locks, the locksmith across from the shop, the way he deactivates the alarm and locks the so-called Japanese perverts in a cell. We also notice the reflection of Rainbow Fashion in the locksmith's window. Again, at the return to the Sonata Café, the gate is closed with a padlock, and the padlock is again associated with Rainbow Fashion through the bag in which he carries the rented costume.

Following Kubrick's logic, we have here a character, Millich, who prostitutes his daughter, rents costumes and masks for ritual parties, and is, through symbolic associations, connected to a network of security and information in the heart of New York. The streets and breweries bear his name, as does the medical colleague of Dr. Harford's office.

"Image 1"

"Image 2"

"Image 3"

"Image 4"

"Image 5"

The character of Millich, through his assigned attitude, is depicted as a blackmailer at the intersection of power and the mafia, with an established presence on the street. He is both protected by and a protector of a well-oiled system, as demonstrated by his nonchalance in the scene where Bill returns the costume, where Millich is not the least bit concerned about thanking his Japanese clients and even offering his daughter's services to the good Doctor. The scene where Ziegler refers to Millich with the phrase "you know who" seems to reinforce this notoriety. The surveillance system, therefore, recalls the one already exposed in *A Clockwork Orange* and this time integrates the technological aspect.

Indeed, it is easy to notice the presence of security systems and their parallel with the dominant sect in the following comparison, clearly visible in the similarity between the throne on which the master of ceremonies sits and the sphere above the surveillance camera at Somerton, suggesting centralized control of the surveillance network. During Bill's visit to the hospital, we see a security guard at the reception desk monitoring cameras, serving as a reminder that says: we have an eye on you.

"Image 1"

"Image 2"

Indeed, the possibility of a mafia-controlled system might shock some, especially in 1999, but it is now well-known that the mafia exerts political control. Let's delve deeper into the analysis and, as before, step out of the film to gain a better understanding.

"Image 3"

Our research leads us to a single character, John Miller in New York, who perfectly fits the profile. He is the son of a journalist and best friend of New York Mafia boss Frank Costello. Until the release of *Eyes Wide Shut*, Miller himself was a journalist for ABC, notably negotiating the interview with Osama Bin Laden. Following this, he served as the spokesperson for the NYPD, eventually becoming the deputy director of Public Affairs at the FBI, managing a significant portion of anti-terrorist intelligence in the post-World Trade Center years. He has been heavily criticized for the FBI and NSA's positions on the surveillance of American citizens but was never truly troubled.

In 2002, Miller married Emily Altschul, an heiress to a branch of the Goldman Sachs/Lehman Brothers bankers, connecting him to the extensive family of Rothschild and Jewish bankers in America and Europe.

Did Kubrick identify Miller, with his connections to the mafia, banks, media, police, and FBI, as the chief watchdog long ago? Given the connections and experiences that preceded this, it is highly plausible. This public servant seems to protect the entire family through his ties with the police and the media.

Sandor, big boss; Freudenstein, Keystone?

"Image 1"

Sandor Szavost, a character with the allure of Aldebaran, leaves a lasting impression primarily through his first name. Sandor makes a grand entrance, projecting an image of someone who thrives on transgression—seducing a married woman and moving freely through his host's property. He introduces himself as a Hungarian with a charismatic, "vampiric" nobility, quoting Latin authors and flaunting his many connections in the art world. Sandor does not tolerate Alice's refusal, although she is visibly captivated by his power, but stops short of betraying her gentle doctor husband, which would have given Sandor full control.

Sandor does not reappear in *Eyes Wide Shut*, except possibly masked at Somerton, yet Kubrick clearly suggests that he is the pinnacle of the mental control hierarchy. No one stands above this character, as Kubrick intended us to understand. Now, we need to step out of the film again to explore the leads offered.

Researching Hungarian Americans named Sandor, aside from György Sándor Ligeti, a composer for the film, and considering Kubrick's Jewish-Hungarian origins, his connections to the music world, his doctor father, as well as themes of chemistry and technology, a few notable figures emerge.

The first, Gyorgi Sandor, was a 20th-century Hungarian pianist and music professor, a student of Bela Bartok and Zoltan Kodaly—the inventor of the Kodaly method of music education (DoReMi) and known for his piano transcriptions of Goethe's *The Sorcerer's Apprentice*. He worked for the Army Signal Corps and U.S. intelligence during World War II, linking him to communication technologies.

The second, George Sandor, possibly a descendant of Gyorgi, is a Harvard and MIT graduate in electronic chemical products and lithium. Beginning his career at FMC, a giant in chemicals for agriculture, aerospace, food, medical, and industrial ventilation systems, he managed contracts related to air conditioning and water treatment. A conspiracy theorist might imagine an industry aimed at magnetizing the population through chemtrails, potable water, air conditioning, and food. However, I wouldn't have focused on George Sandor, risking defamation, if I hadn't stumbled upon his name in Ferdinand Freudenstein's Wikipedia article, identifying him as Sandor's mentor and already mentioned Kay Freudenstein's uncle.

Ferdinand Freudenstein is a legend in modern physics, known for modern kinematics and simplified equations for electromagnetic waves and frequencies. Born to the Freudenstein/Rosenberg couple, a Jewish family in Germany in 1926, Ferdinand and his brother fled to England before he settled in New York, founding the Freudenstein academic lineage. His brother established the powerful Freudenstein dynasty in Australia.

As a Columbia professor, Ferdinand provided radio frequency consulting for Bell Telephone Labs, IBM, and General Motors. His simplified calculation methods likely saved computing resources, allowing for simultaneity in an AI-automated analysis system.

In the Australian branch, Richard Freudenstein, a major fortune, has a rich CV: former director of numerous media, radio broadcasting, sports, digital services, and boards of major food retailers like Foxtel, Sky News, News Digital Media, News Corp, Cricket Australia, and Coles.

His wife, Jane, involved in various NGOs and charities, serves on boards like the Sydney Children Hospital Foundation and The Australian Ballet. Lastly, Kay Freudenstein-Hayes, previously mentioned, is a former KPMG consultant, News Corp's global IT system project manager, and now head of IT at Uniting ACT.NSW. This organization and family, with ties to media, justice, and police, are unassailable. Kay also serves as vice-president of Willoughby Council (Chatswood), one of Sydney's wealthiest areas, and on the board of NSW Art Gallery, whose 2022 program, designed by Kay, presents the societal vision prepared by this family.

I've witnessed this organization's establishment of sham juries protecting many pedophiles and traffickers like international child trafficker Beau Lamarre-Condon, an NSW juvenile police officer and "star blogger," shielded by Australian justice connections (Judge Stein) and the selection of jurors from corrupted Uniting employees. Lamarre-Condon assassinated two media figures about to expose him, connected to Australia's space program, Wildenstein Gardens, the Stein family, and Charlise Mutten's murder.

Conversations with Michelle Simon and Kay Freudenstein confirmed a certain level of inbreeding within these families, occasionally exchanging in Yiddish. Michelle Simon once said, "the bad guys always win." Without proof, I believe Uniting and this network protect a child trafficking and mental control programming organization, at minimum serving as informants for isolated prey, at worst, profiting themselves. This corroborates Kubrick's entire filmography and Barnett's *Eyes Wide Open*.

A simple solution to prevent these abuses is creating a global public communication line, rather than leaving infiltrated states to manage these systems. Only publicity and citizen action can protect against these ritual abuses, highlighting the importance of maintaining platforms like Twitter.

Image 1: Ferdinand Freudenstein

Image 2 : Kay Freudenstein-Hayes

Image 3 : Richard Freudenstein

Image 4 : Jane Freudenstein

Image 4 : Rupert Murdoch

Image 5 : Michelle Simon
Uniting NSW.ACT

The ideal Society according to Kay Freudenstein, extract from the Art Gallery of NSW 2022 Program (public document)

Coincidences are multiplying... The character of Sandor points us again towards various fields: chemistry (George Sandor), radio communications (Gyorgi Sandor and Ferdinand Freudenstein), community and childhood services (Kay Freudenstein), and the media (Richard Freudenstein). Thus, the constellation of key actors in mental control expands: Simon, Freudenstein, Miller, and Sandor. These public faces are likely supported by the British Crown and subcontracting organizations for public services, originally focused on radio communications, as discussed in our analysis of *The Shining*: SERCO.

Was it Kubrick's intention to point us toward Australia by choosing Nicole Kidman as an actress? Could the underground bunkers mentioned in *Dr. Strangelove* be in Australia or New Zealand, not far from the South Pole? Isn't Australia one of the keys to the Five Eyes cooperation, particularly with the American base Pine Gap? Aren't its universities, especially Sydney University, heavily funded by the CIA and the American military? Could Australia be a testing ground for the deep state, closely linked with Hollywood through its studios and broadcasting equipment? Have the various space agencies, under the guise of space exploration, ultimately focused all their efforts on establishing this global mental control system? Who are all these vampires, and how do we get rid of them?

Many questions yet to be answered.

STOP CMB - A Discovery Confirming Our Intuitions

As Bill realizes he is being followed, he is refused by several taxis, and we can see a STOP sign tagged with the acronym CMB.

Here we simultaneously observe two things: the influence of an artificially induced negative karma and the STOP CMB sign, referencing the Cosmic Microwave Background mentioned earlier, suggesting a connection.

This detail hints at Kubrick's meticulous use of symbols to convey deeper meanings, tying the concept of universal vibrations and frequencies into the narrative. It appears that Kubrick is subtly pointing towards the idea that our reality and experiences might be manipulated through cosmic manipulations. The STOP CMB sign, therefore, serves as a warning or an indicator of the control exerted by these evil forces over the technology, calling back to the 2001: A

Space Odyssey and the learned apes in addition to the key players we have just mentioned. Note that Dr Floyd also reports to Miller.

"Image 1"

In "Eyes Wide Shut," we see multiple examples of what the karma/machine might be capable of: taxis rudely refusing Bill's fare; conversely, the hotel receptionist and Sally being very friendly. Through vibrational action, it seems the Wizard of Oz can positively or negatively adjust Dr. Harford's interactions. Some might say that this is simply how karma works; fair enough, it would be hard for me to prove otherwise.

Are we all becoming robots controlled by a microwave machine located at the South Pole, or as described in NATO's new military doctrine, a cognitive weapon with directed energy? Was this technology tested by the United States on its own men during the Havana Syndrome incident? Has the CIA taken control of it, or have they lost control over it? What is Australia's role in all this? And what about the Wizard of Oz?

More questions arise...

Summary

"Eyes Wide Shut" serves as Kubrick's cosmology and ritual, a true initiation into the universe's secrets and a warning against imminent changes. It portrays malevolent and mafia-like forces that control media, surveillance, blackmail, and corruption, having likely seized global mental control through microwave weapons orchestrated by AI and a military-scientific consortium, with NASA and certain secret operations probably based at the poles, aided by the pharmaceutical and food industries.

Kubrick attempts to make humanity a family of initiates, warning against CMB research. He clearly exposes Freemasonry as the iceberg's visible part of control while pointing to the submerged actors we've mentioned earlier.

The Ziegler House relates to the event forgers as described by James Tilly Matthews, with official protection from Carleton Simon, suggesting a close link between New York and Sydney based on our analysis.

The global oligarchy, through its black magic, seeks to turn humanity into a family of golems at its service. This sets the stage for our transition to "Lolita," which already in 1962 exposed the control of universities by the Epstein network, or its predecessors.

CHAPTER 6
Lolita

Fleeing, a smooth talker he now fashions himself a sage.
But Lolita, to her new stepfather, aims for the stage.
To Epstein, ancient producer, at Mexican mansions engage,
Sold her soul to Evil - Sue Lyon seeks a paternal page.

In the upcoming chapters, we will further explore and expand upon the themes already discussed, refining our understanding of Kubrick's intentions and methods of expression. It will be emphasized that he spent his life trying to expose deep state.

In the 1962 film "Lolita," University professor Humbert Humbert (played by James Mason) falls in love with a 14-year-old girl named Dolores Haze, also known as "Lolita" (portrayed by Sue Lyon). Humbert becomes obsessed with Lolita and, after marrying her mother, tries everything to get closer to her. "Lolita" is an adaptation of the eponymous novel by Vladimir Nabokov, who also wrote the screenplay for the film.

As is his custom, under the guise of dark comedy, Kubrick exposes and juxtaposes two real forms of paedophilia. The first is the "everyday paedophilia" of the untalented professor Humbert Humbert, which takes place in homes and presents itself as an impossible and ambiguous love story that does more harm to the man who practices it than to the young victim, who plays with her influence and the protection of the community to manipulate him.

The other form is the paedophilia is one of the Quilty network, which deals with manipulation and money, a character played by Peter Sellers, just like Dr. Strangelove, and who recalls without difficulty the Epstein network. This network of paedophilia, which has a storefront thanks to media support and Quilty's fortune, clearly has access to schools and informants.

Once again, it seems that our main character, naive and too human, walks on two legs, like a golem, into a web of control that had been set up to protect a network of vices and trafficking, invisible to the eyes of the professor, a network of which he himself becomes the scapegoat: an orthodox husband in insurances, dead in strange circumstances, lawyer friends with liberated morals, a series of trips to Mexico by the widow, the premature death of the latter and this omnipresent and omnipotent Quilty chameleon.

We find again and always the themes dear to Kubrick: the shattered family, the materialistic society and power, the hospital and psychiatry, satanic rituals, vices, and women. As usual, he dares to identify the places and actors of the criminal network, a ranch in New Mexico where Quilty, this timeless master blackmailer, organizes his control of the high society of entertainment, the army, and politics, in short, the veneer.

Humbert the Golem

"Image 1"

"Image 2"

Through his ambiguous relationship and behaviour, Humbert is both a victim and a culprit of the network that facilitates the exploitation of the young girl. Indeed, his foolishness makes him a perfect golem, led by the nose by little Lolita and by the Quilty network, who can use him as a scapegoat or fall guy if Lolita decides to publicly expose the network. Like "Eyes Wide Shut," from the moment Humbert arrives at Dolores's house, he is surrounded, followed, and watched by agents or watchdogs serving the network, and he definitively compromises himself when he spends the night in the same hotel room as the young girl, while a police convention is taking place in the hotel, suggesting the complicity of the police.

This golem thesis is strongly reinforced by the Frankenstein scene, representing that infamous golem out of control. In Jewish mysticism and mythology, the golem is an artificial being made of clay brought to life, incapable of speech and devoid of free will, created to assist or defend its creator. This perfectly fits the character of Humbert, whose free will is annihilated by his subjugation to Lolita.

His love for Lolita places him in an uncontrollable forward flight resulting in his psychological and material ruin, his downfall marked by a form of paranoia, jealousy, and obsession for revenge on Quilty, which is a projection of his own demons. He seems to be chasing his shadow, as evidenced by the final scene where he seeks out Quilty, reinforced by the scene where Quilty reads Humbert's redundant letter, mocking Humbert's lament over Quilty taking advantage of him. Poor Humbert, mocks Quilty.

If Humbert is primarily the golem of the exploitation network, he is ultimately the golem of the beautiful and cruel Lolita, who delivers a form of divine punishment for his naivety and foolishness. In the scene where he visits a pregnant Lolita, while he still can redeem himself and show kindness to the couple or simply disinterest; Humbert, presumptuous and blind professor of French literature and amateur poet lacking philosophy, still believes he can save Lolita from the vile network for which he is himself shamefully responsible. However, he will obtain what he came for, the opportunity to avenge his own demons, rather than integrating them.

Indeed, it seems that this old adolescent never truly reached adulthood.

Peter Sellers and Clare Quilty

Clare Quilty, a screenwriter by nature, is a storyteller, the key character through whom Kubrick conveys most of his message. Manipulative, he alternates roles throughout the film, painting the constellation of a network of sexual exploitation of minors: he is alternately a theatre and film director for Hollywood who mingles with the community and the common people, a high-ranking policeman attending a convention, and a high school psychologist diagnosing Lolita.

Through these different characters all played by the genius Peter Sellers, the gears of the deep state are revealed. The successful screenwriter makes headlines, holds conferences in country clubs and Rotary clubs, and his uncle is a well-respected community dentist, particularly among women. Here, a theme very similar to that of "Eyes Wide Shut" emerges, but in a suburban version, where control and trafficking are exercised through women and vice.

The opening scene, presenting Humbert Humbert seeking revenge on Quilty, who seems to have completely forgotten him and mistakes him for an army captain, immediately suggests Quilty's high-level connections. He lives in a mansion and is surrounded by material wealth, leading a life of debauchery, gambling, and alcohol. Awoken from a drunken stupor by his visitor, he makes numerous references to the Roman Empire and power but never seems concerned about the immorality of his actions: from his point of view, he has done nothing wrong or immoral—it's all just a simple game to him.

When threatened with a gun, he says: "We're in a house of good people, and you are either Australian or a German refugee." Is Kubrick suggesting that Quilty is a goy and had certain rivalries with Australians and Germans? He also says: "Captain, are you here for the Ranch title?" implying the New Mexico ranch where political blackmail, rituals, and wild parties are organized, as Lolita will later mention, was a contested and likely coveted territory by certain members of the military-industrial complex.

Following this, Quilty, understanding that Humbert is not there for material interest but out of love, tries by all means to negotiate his life with various forms of payment: composing a piece of music together (success), paying him (money), offering him women (sex), giving him his house, using his friends as furniture (power, cf. the orgy in "Eyes Wide Shut"), or even offering a group of people to sacrifice (satanism). Thus, we understand that for Clare Quilty, everything is for sale, from the arts to the darkest vices, and he knows their market value.

Peter Sellers represents all the links in this network: show business, police, and psychiatry.

Drawing of an Ourobouros

The single-parent family

Charlotte Haze, the desperate and despairing single mother, will leave the door open to any decent man, exposing her own daughter to the wolf. The single mother suffers from the shadow that her daughter casts on her, and her neurosis only becomes more and more apparent with age.

One can wonder how, unoccupied and dreaming of a prince charming, a widowed or separated woman will arrive serenely at the twilight of her life, putting herself in jealous competition with her own daughter who will flee at the first opportunity, for success, money or muscles.

If Humbert appears more as a smitten lover and a cursed poet than as a sexual predator, he nevertheless lacks philosophy and emotional control and lets himself being manipulated by the little Lolita who, for her part, does not lack a judge's daughter to pull her pin out of the game.

Charlotte Haze will die of madness after discovering Humbert's diary, at the reading of his buried impulses for Lolita, virtual but real betrayal, which recalls Alice's confession of the fantasy in EWS and what follows.

Humbert seems satisfied with the event; he himself becomes the single parent of Lolita and will be able to have Lolita to himself... It is true that the charm of the hormonal emanations of a faded materialist flower does not compare to those of Lolita, a young flower freshly bloomed and dreamy, nevertheless he's now cursed and guilty.

The ex-husband

"Image 1"

The religious altar erected for the late husband symbolizes societal values: the upright husband was worth more dead than alive. It is clearly suggested here that this altar is not a tribute to the deceased but rather an altar to the insurance money that came with his death, leaving the widow in substantial material comfort. This is indicated by the placement of his photo in the position of God, above the orthodox altar dedicated to Jesus Christ.

It seems likely that a network, exploiting Mrs. Haze's foolishness and the deceased husband's lack of vigilance and defensive measures—being over-insured and insufficiently protected—could have orchestrated his death for profit by various means: legal fees, the widow's excessive spending, exploitation of her daughter, and the elimination of a contradictory and bothersome moral authority that the orthodox deceased husband probably represented.

The Swingers

"Image 1"

From the moment Humbert arrives at the school dance, he is approached by a couple whose liberated practices seem quite evident. This couple is close to Mrs. Haze and it is clear they exert a certain power over this lone woman. One might wonder if they had any role in the death of the previous "upright" husband, who, being a fervent believer, likely had little in common with this charming couple and was worth more dead than alive. The husband presents himself as a lawyer who is also present at Mrs. Haze's death.

The offer made to Humbert in this inappropriate setting gives an impression of rampant madness and a decadent, absurd society, reinforced by the presence of Quilty and his sinister wife. The school is depicted here as a place of debauchery, not for the children but for their parents. They prepare themselves, seeking escapism, thrills, and direction. A new arrival is a potential source of distraction and personal gain, be it material or chemical.

This couple of power, inclined towards swinging and closely connected to the legal system, suggests a corrupt administration that acts as a guardian of a lucrative network of various traffics.

Dr. Zymph

Dr. Zymph, the school psychologist, is one of the characters played by Peter Sellers. With his German accent and dominant demeanour due to his position of power, he, like all Sellers' characters in the film, represents a link in the chain controlling the juvenile prostitution network that ensnares Lolita. From his dominant position, after providing a Freudian clinical diagnosis of Lolita's "excessive libido repression," for which he holds Humbert responsible, Dr. Zymph gives Humbert an ultimatum: either open his home to an inspection by four psychologists or allow Lolita to participate in extracurricular activities, specifically the school play directed by Quilty. We later learn that this was all orchestrated by Quilty, who persuaded Humbert to let Lolita go due to his guilt.

Humbert, isolated against this network and guilty of his love for Lolita, cannot defend himself and is forced to hand her over to the network, becoming the fool in the situation as her legal guardian. The rest of Lolita's social network—including school officials, social services, psychologists, and parents—conspire to deliver the now orphaned pretty young girl to powerful men, likely in exchange for political and financial favours. Why should Humbert be the only one to enjoy this rare gem? It turns out that Lolita, deeply infatuated with Quilty and his success, was complicit in the deception. She mentions his "Japanese-style Oriental spirituality," or something similar, which reminds us of the Masonic rite of the Grand Orient and Millich's Japanese clients in Eyes Wide Shut.

The various characters portrayed by Peter Sellers, including Dr. Zymph, represent this informational and professional network that identifies and isolates easy preys and their irresponsible, manipulable, or docile guardians. Another depiction of the medical and psychiatric network is the scene where Humbert, her legal guardian, comes to fetch Lolita from the hospital. This highlights his total helplessness against the network. Drunk, Humbert is threatened with a straitjacket by the hospital staff, while earlier, Quilty had likely taken Lolita to the Mexican ranch. Humbert is cornered and cannot oppose Lolita's will, having no real moral authority.

This dreamer is doubly humiliated by Lolita and the entire community, which holds him responsible for the whole thing.

"Image 1"

The Quilty network, the New Mexico ranch, and the Epstein network

The last meeting between Humbert and Lolita lifts the veil on the Quilty network's method: promising young girls' success in Hollywood while mobilizing rich and powerful perverts willing to pay or compromise to satisfy their fantasies. Lolita specifies the place and method: a ranch in New Mexico where painters, bodybuilders, and other artists film their sexual experiments, in exchange for money or benefits.

It is suggested many times that Lolita's mother is herself part of the network, consciously or unconsciously: the very dubious death of her "honest" husband who left her a nice inheritance, her pronounced taste for Mexico and her fascination with Quilty suggest that she is herself manipulated by the network that eliminated her husband and her in what may not be a simple accident, to leave Lolita to herself and free to consume.

This network reminds us all too well of the Epstein/Maxwell network that has been making a lot of noise in recent years. This network, which attracted young women and teenage girls through its modelling network, promised them mountains and wonders in exchange for their favours with powerful men. Ghislaine Maxwell, daughter of press and political magnate Robert Maxwell (Daily Mail), close to British and Israeli intelligence services, buried on the Mount of Olives in Jerusalem, operated with Epstein a system of blackmail control of politicians, scientists, artists and received characters such as Stephen Hawking or Bill Gates on numerous occasions.

"Image 1: Epstein Ranch, New-Mexico"

The duo Rob Maxwell /Alistair Campbell still points to Australia, Campbell being the director of the board of Orygen organization which replaced that of the late Anthony Kidman.

If Epstein's Island developed a certain reputation for hosting characters such as Bill Clinton or Bill Gates, he had a ranch built in 1997 in New Mexico under the name of Zorro Ranch where part of the trafficking and fine parties operated. The film Lolita, released in 1960, therefore already evokes a very similar place and we can legitimately ask since when this network has been operating and if this is not a timeless network, of which Epstein was the operator for about twenty years but which exists with or without him, emanation of a deep state and deeply mafioso intelligence services in their operation.

Let us note that the Epstein organization operated under the cover of modelling agencies which served as recruiters and applied methods very similar to those described here: promising and preparing success for young girls who were then used to blackmail key players and extort information. These agencies had their ramifications in France, through Ghislaine Maxwell and Jean-Luc Brunel, also dead in prison after his arrest for paedophilia, just like Jeffrey Epstein.

If Epstein was a blackmailer with psychopathic traits who loved very young women and was mixed with the deep American and Israeli power, it is not obvious that this network was the only one or the most extreme in its practices.

We have been too quick to pass Epstein off as a paedophile to hide the ramifications of his very extensive network in finance, science and technology. Indeed, what interest for a pervert to gather all these skills, other than power and control over a technology of which we may not yet have knowledge?

CHAPTER 7
Dr Srangelove (1964)

Nuclear Apocalypse is shed from induced madness and suggestions casted
To a mundane Scapegoat, Admiral protecting vital pineal gland,
Saved shall be chosen ones by Dr Semite or Nazi Noah,
And by magic bunkers, rations and women: the Australian Ark.

Doctor Strangelove or: How I Learned to Stop Worrying and Love the Bomb tells the story of an American general portrayed as psychotic who initiates a nuclear attack against the Soviet Union without consulting the President. The ensuing negotiations between the American and Russian high commands aim to avoid the nuclear apocalypse that would result from the Soviet Union's new, automatic, and unstoppable weapon. The film takes place in three main locations: a locked-down base from which General Ripper launches the nuclear attack, the cockpit of the B-52 tasked with dropping the atomic bomb, and the Pentagon War Room.

While the plot ostensibly presents a clash between Russian communists and American imperialists, Kubrick, as usual, portrays a much more complex and nuanced situation, incorporating elements that were not yet publicly known at the time: the existence of a Nazi-inspired scientific lobby within the American government (Project Paperclip), the existence of a Jewish communist lobby in the United States represented by actor Peter Sellers, and finally, the power of various industries and financial forces, particularly the food and military-industrial industries that influence the media, mystique, and organize global mind control: New York Times and Coca-Cola.

This film, considered by many to be one of the greatest black comedies ever made, was released at the height of the Vietnam War and still harbors a few secrets that we will attempt to uncover here.

The film presents three key settings. An American base locked-down from which General Ripper launches the nuclear attack represents the unilateral and unchecked power wielded by certain military officials, the cockpit of a B-52 Nuclear bomber scenes emphasizes the human element within the machinery of war, and the Pentagon War Room that illustrates the bureaucratic and absurd nature of high-stakes decision-making during a nuclear crisis.

Kubrick's portrayal of the power dynamics goes beyond the surface-level Cold War dichotomy. The film hints at the influence of a Nazi-inspired scientific lobby within the American government, an allusion to the real-life Operation Paperclip, where former Nazi scientists were recruited by the US. This element suggests a lingering and problematic influence of former enemy ideologies within American institutions.

The presence of a Jewish communist lobby in the US, represented by Peter Sellers, introduces another layer of complexity, highlighting the internal ideological battles and the diverse influences shaping American policy during the Cold War.

The influence of the military-industrial complex and the role of industries like food and media in shaping public perception and policy are also central themes. Coca-Cola and the New York Times symbolize the intertwined interests of business and government in controlling the narrative and influencing global politics.

"Image 1"

Nuclear Bombs and Zhokhov Island

When *Dr. Strangelove* was released in 1964, it wasn't public knowledge that the Soviets had built an apocalyptic weapon capable of annihilating the world. This weapon, revealed to the public in 1984 under the name "Perimeter," is an "automatic" dormant weapon designed, according to nuclear military doctrine, to deter an adversary from launching an attack. If the adversary were to launch such an attack, Perimeter would automatically trigger an unstoppable retaliatory strike, much like the scenario described in *Dr. Strangelove*.

The film was mocked and attacked upon its release, likely because almost everything in it was true: the Soviet doomsday weapon, the delegation of authority to use nuclear weapons to generals and officers, the functioning of high commands, control systems, military procedures, the B-52 cockpit transporting the American nuclear warhead, and even the recruitment of former Nazis within American military intelligence.

We are at the heart of the Cold War and the central problem it posed. It is highly probable that *Dr. Strangelove* theorized and popularized nuclear doctrine for millions of viewers, while highlighting the absurdity of the arms race and its risks. The film likely played a role in President Kennedy's modifications to nuclear regulations in the early 1960s to secure transport, use, and command rules, thus avoiding risky delegations of authority.

Regarding Zhokhov Island in the Siberian Arctic, there is no evidence that Soviet nuclear weapons were installed there, except perhaps in one of their nuclear submarines. Knowing Kubrick and aligning with the theory of mind control through food and magnetism, one might consider the track of Commander Zhukov, a namesake of the island. Zhukov was a commander and political leader in the Soviet army who maintained cordial relations with Eisenhower as they toured the Soviet Union together after World War II. The anecdote tells that Eisenhower introduced Zhukov to Coca-Cola, and to avoid being seen as a traitor for consuming American products, Zhukov made a special order for White Coke (Clear Coke).

B-52, CRM 114, and Radio Communication

The cockpit and military procedures of the B-52 bomber were so accurately reproduced in *Dr. Strangelove* that Kubrick faced accusations of espionage. However, it turns out he simply drew inspiration from a photograph and military manuals.

The B-52 crew is depicted as being under a form of mental control: they pass their time snacking and reading Playboy. It was originally intended for the Texan character, who ultimately rides the bomb, to be played by Peter Sellers. However, Sellers declined due to the already numerous roles he was playing in the film. From Kubrick's perspective, this Texan is one of the "bad guys."

Kubrick highlights the practical aspects and potential pitfalls of a military operation carried out outside of an exercise context, emphasizing the dependence of all participants on information technology, operators for the transmission and execution of orders.

How can such a military operation be conducted when communications are sometimes intercepted by the enemy, and powers and authorities are poorly distributed? This touches on the core problem that drives elites to seek to transform humans into machines and control them remotely.

In such a critical context as the operation of nuclear weapons, it is challenging to rely on human beings and their emotional states, although some individuals, like the Texan, display unwavering zeal resulting from thorough conditioning. Moreover, one cannot fully rely on technology, which can sometimes fail or be hacked, as is the case with the CRM 114 device, intended to transmit the recall order to the crew, or more recently, the widespread outage of Microsoft operating systems.

From the elite's perspective, eliminating human risk is a necessary element in managing the world, making the risk exclusively technological and, to some extent, more controllable. However, machines are themselves built and programmed by humans. This logic drives us toward a programmatic world akin to *The Matrix*, a sort of simulation of reality that has little to do with actual reality, or worse, toward a reality dictated by machines. The B-52 cockpit and CRM 114 are thus a prelude to the next evolution towards HAL 9000 or ChatGPT.

The CRM 114 radio receiver reappears in A Clockwork Orange as Serum 114, which is injected into Alex by his psychiatrist. Does this suggest that Serum 114 is the cure for human weakness, turning humans into radios that can receive messages or be remotely?

The communists

In Dr. Strangelove, the Soviets are represented by the Russian ambassador, who has access to the Pentagon through the American President and his phone calls to the USSR President. The Soviets are depicted as equals to the Americans in every way: they enjoy Cuban cigars, good food, and beautiful women. The Russian President, always drinking vodka, doesn't seem hostile towards the Americans and appears to want to maintain cordial relations. However, his reaction is understandably negative upon learning that a bomber is heading towards Moscow.

The ambassador eventually mentions the various races that the United States is pushing Russia into the arms race, the space race, the race for cinema and culture, all of which hinder social development, the supposed raison d'être of communism or socialism. It seems these competitions and mutual psychoses do not emanate from the state itself but are driven by the New York Times.

Again, Kubrick highlights the theme of mystique, media, and private agents as the root causes of divisions and conflicts. These entities are capable of swaying public opinion and forging events and rivalries, forcing everyone into a great competition from which no one emerges victorious, except for few silent industrialists in the War Room.

Kubrick indirectly shows an America that, while defining itself as "imperialist," is already overtaken by communism in that it has become a massive bureaucracy with its telephone standards, lack of leadership, "cooperation with the enemy," slowness, and parasites.

Kubrick suggests that communism, before being a chosen ideology, is a natural emanation of human organizations, a consequence of bureaucracies. These organizations, ostensibly meant for the allocation of collective resources, end up serving only themselves.

Thus, attacking communism, as General Ripper attempts to, is for a military man, a state functionary, akin to attacking oneself. This is literally shown when Ripper locks down his base and orders his men to shoot any approaching Americans, hilariously illustrating a complex concept that only Kubrick could convey so well.

The confrontation between communists and imperialists is a sham, a media storytelling that allows industries and science, personified by Dr. Strangelove and the generals in the War Room, to expand and display their power while testing their mind control systems. It is strongly suggested, as in *The Shining*, that on a scientific and military line, the Soviets and Americans are two sides of the same coin, interested in maintaining a perpetual war.

Kubrick's *Dr. Strangelove* thus reveals the absurdity and inherent contradictions within Cold War politics and the bureaucratic systems of both superpowers, highlighting the manipulative power of media and the underlying unity between supposed ideological adversaries.

Ripper the Samurai, Mandrake the Poison, and the Fluid Theory

General Jack D. Ripper, whose name references the infamous serial killer Jack the Ripper, is a character who today might be labelled as a "conspiracy theorist" or a "toxic male" in modern jargon, and he bears some resemblance to Colonel Kurtz from *Apocalypse Now*. Like Kurtz, Ripper embraces an oriental spirituality. He locks down his base to launch a nuclear attack on Russia, claiming his country has been infiltrated by communists who are polluting the water with fluoride, advocating for the protection of his vital fluids. The conspiracy theory of water fluoridation by communists was prevalent in the 1950s.

General Ripper: A Misunderstood Figure?

Ripper epitomizes the American military archetype: a tall, strong man smoking a cigar, paternalistic towards his men, with a deep voice, exaggerated virility, numerous decorations and combat achievements, and a love of firearms. At first glance, it seems Kubrick portrays this character negatively and mocks him, as indicated by his name and his outlandish speeches that might be mistaken for paranoid schizophrenia. Indeed, Ripper has an internal conflict: he is unknowingly attacking himself. Note that actor Sterling Hayden, who played Ripper, was himself a communist who fought alongside Yugoslav partisans during World War II and was even decorated by Marshal Tito, reinforcing the idea of collusion between the two camps.

One might be inclined to think Ripper is mentally disturbed, especially given the contemporary portrayal of fluoride in water as a ridiculous conspiracy theory. Today, it is known that fluoride can have detrimental effects on the brain, memory, and intuition as it causes calcification of the pineal gland, also known as the third eye, which Kubrick frequently references in his films. Like HAL9000 in *2001*, Ripper is a human character with the intuition of an impending great evil but fails to identify its source, driving him to launch the nuclear attack.

Mandrake: The Real Threat?

Peter Sellers plays Mandrake, who also portrayed the demonic network characters in *Lolita*, as well as the eponymous mad scientist Dr. Strangelove and the relatively weak President of the United States. Mandrake initially appears more sympathetic and benevolent than Sellers' other characters, but this is another Kubrickian illusion.

Mandrake's name references the hallucinogenic and magical plant mandrake, whose root, shaped like a man, is said to scream when uprooted. Readers of *Harry Potter* will be familiar with this. Initially presented as a pretentious character surrounded by computers and specializing in calculations rather than field warfare, Mandrake is the opposite of General Ripper in every way: a small, undecorated, cowardly, and volatile Englishman, disrespectful of authority and abusive of his own. He is possibly himself a communist, perhaps unwittingly. These clues (the actor Peter Sellers, Mandrake's name, and his character traits) suggest that while Kubrick mocks Ripper, it is Mandrake and what he represents that is the deeper cause of Ripper's irreversible decision to launch the attack on Russia.

The hallucinogenic mandrake plant quietly spreads its poison throughout American administrations, reaching the highest levels of government, as confirmed by the President's character, who is a sort of advanced stage Mandrake, and whom one might imagine screaming if uprooted. Mandrake prefigures the swift transformation of warfare from being conducted by violent, virile, courageous, and stupid men to being waged by pretentious and vicious "nerds" specializing in information and politics, a specialty of the British Crown and its secret services. This is evident in Mandrake's introduction, reading computer tapes.

Ripper, as a true soldier willing to sacrifice, goes to the end of his soul to defend his country, as evidenced by his well-executed plan and subsequent suicide to avoid certain torture aimed at cancelling the nuclear attack, further proving his high level of prediction and deduction. Ripper might be the only truly lucid character in the film, with his theory on the purity of fluids being a reality unknown to all but inferred by his strong intuition, spiritual capacity, and empirical nature, driving him to drink rainwater. This theory might seem delusional and incomprehensible to the uninitiated, such as the viewers, who are already rendered stupid by their consumption of tap water, lack of physical activity, careless ejaculation, consumption of fluoridated chewing gum, and media exposure.

Mandrake, who seems physically and spiritually ill, suffers from tendonitis and lacks courage, honour, and a sense of sacrifice, yet he appears happy. Repeatedly, details cleverly placed by Kubrick show Mandrake, like General Buck, chewing gum. Furthermore, the phone booth scene where Captain Guano says, "If you can't reach the President, you'll have to answer to the Coca-Cola Company (a private entity)," informs us about the true rulers of the United States while correcting Ripper's error.

Thus, while Ripper does not mistake the fight, he might mistake the enemy, like Humbert the golem, by designating communism as the source of his woes, whereas Kubrick seems to point towards private enterprises like Coca-Cola, chewing gum producers, or the military-industrial complex. The communists are not presented as the monsters Ripper imagines, especially since he smokes the same cigars as they do. But Ripper lacks the patience to play the political game to assert his view and plays his one and only card to save his country and its values, like a samurai in a final assault. Regardless of one's thoughts on his action, one cannot help but feel a certain sympathy for Ripper, unlike the other degenerate and lustful military archetypes.

Kubrick masterfully deceives the audience into believing he portrays Ripper as a psychotic madman while he is the only character to have identified the existential threat to the United States. However, if Ripper is intuitive, unlike HAL9000, he does not possess omniscient knowledge and mistakes the enemy. Remember, Kubrick is a chess player; to reveal the truth, facing deep power, he must mock it and hide it, with the details shedding light on his true perspective.

From *Dr. Strangelove* onwards, Kubrick informs us about the magnetization of fluids serving the deep state in the application of soft power and potentially serves early mind control research. In this context, is the reference to Commander Zokhov truly anecdotal?

Guano: The Dual-Industry Key

To confirm theories about the food and military industries, here's a synthesis: Captain Guano.

Guano, a product derived from bird and bat droppings, is used in two industries: agriculture as fertilizer and the military as an explosive. This character, therefore, provides us with a key to understanding: the food and military industries are one and the same, an industry to which he himself, despite sporting grenades on his jacket, does not wish to get too close.

"Image 1 : Guano and Coca Cola"

Operation Paperclip and Dr. Strangelove

Operation Paperclip was a secret U.S. operation conducted after World War II to recruit German scientists, engineers, and technicians, especially those involved in Germany's advanced weapons, aeronautics, and space programs. Over 1,600 German experts were brought to the U.S. to work for the American government under false identities. This operation, which lasted from 1945 to 1962, aimed to acquire advanced technological knowledge and prevent these experts from falling into Soviet hands. Some of the recruited scientists had troubling pasts, including affiliations with the Nazi party and accusations of war crimes. The most famous among them was Wernher von Braun, who became the director of the American space program.

Persistent rumours suggest that not all German scientists were repatriated during the operation, with many reportedly fleeing, disappearing, or possibly heading to Latin America or the South Pole via submarine. However, we will not delve into this speculative terrain.

Dr. Strangelove directly references Operation Paperclip. The name "Strangelove" is a nod to the ambiguous love relationship between the United States and the former Nazi war criminals they had supposedly defeated in Germany. Throughout much of the film, Dr. Strangelove observes the farcical situation silently until the point of no return.

Eventually, it is revealed that he oversees research and development for the military, deeply knowledgeable about various technologies and the potential of nuclear and computer automation.

He possesses detailed plans for the elite in the event of a nuclear apocalypse, which would reduce the world's population to 700,000 people whose survival would rely on repurposing old mines and pre-existing bunkers. This plan echoes the globalists' projects under the guise of environmental protection and climate change, imposing absurd, punitive, and untenable regulations on agriculture, housing, and daily consumption, championed by the new Nazis at the WEF, the UN, or the European Commission.

Dr. Strangelove, Dr. Floyd, and Dr. Miller are on a boat, the Australian Ark. And what should we do with it? We should sink it.

CHAPITRE 8
Barry Lyndon (1975)

Grown up, the rancor from incestuous love stain,
Propels him to glory and adventure, seeking to forget the pain.
He plays, he gropes, he cheats, forging his own game,
But the debt beware! It is sickness, without knowledge or reign...

Barry Lyndon is primarily an exploration of the rapid degeneration of a vice-ridden, unbalanced society where the absence of spiritual, religious, and paternal figures leaves social ascension as the only motive for action. It leads to the feminization and homosexualization of men and to the tearing apart of families. In this universal tale about human nature, Barry Lyndon confronts his destiny, experiencing the emotions and sentiments associated with both vices and virtues.

It serves as a moral and ethical treatise, presented as the tragic fictitious biography of a minor 18th-century Irish nobleman clumsily attempting to gain power. Like many of Kubrick's films, it can serve as an example for the youth of what not to follow, akin to Aristotle's bequest to his son, the Nicomachean Ethics, or Homer's Odyssey in its treatment of human relationships and the father-son and mother-son dynamics.

This slow-paced tragicomedy, depicting Barry Lyndon's rise and fall, impresses primarily through its cinematography and technical innovations, making the film a meticulous and timeless masterpiece. Any frame could be extracted and displayed in a classical art museum. Heavily inspired by Renaissance painters and Hogarth's modern moral subjects, the film reveals a new facet of Kubrick as he captures natural and picturesque spaces and attempts to capture the essence of the organization and functioning of the pre-French Revolution European deep state during the Seven Years' War, a pivotal period foreshadowing the new world order that would follow, which Kubrick has taken care to depict in his other films.

This film testifies once again to Kubrick's prudence and his desire to mark the history of art and cinema, elevating it to a major art form while seeking to represent an era of particular importance in understanding the modern and future world, in its complexity and reality, both individual and psychological as well as collective and organizational.

The film is divided into two parts: the first presents the fraudulent rise of Redmond Barry, a minor Irish bourgeois, detailing the glories and shames of youthful recklessness; the second part tells of his downfall, reminiscent of the karmic retribution in A Clockwork Orange, where Barry pays dearly for his ill-gotten gains.

NASA Connexion

"Image 2"

Armstrong on the moon, 1969, Public domain

The legend tells us that Stanley Kubrick had a special camera built to mount a 50mm f/0.7 lens, which he purchased from NASA. This lens, known as the Carl Zeiss Planar, is the fastest lens in the world, with only ten units ever made. Kubrick bought three of these lenses, and they explain the unique look of Barry Lyndon with its natural colors in low light: all interior scenes were filmed by candlelight without additional lighting. These lenses serve as yet another nod to his close relationship with NASA.

Napoleon and Macron

Barry Lyndon doesn't directly address Napoleon, but it's important to remember that Kubrick spent nearly a decade studying and collecting information to make a film about Napoleon, which he ultimately cancelled due to the success of Bondarchuk's Soviet film, *Waterloo*.

Barry's meteoric rise within the English nobility through his military exploits and ambition can be seen as reminiscent of the rise Napoleon might have needed for his campaign. Napoleon, the Italian who took control of France during the Revolution and transformed it into an Empire, only to face a disastrous fall against Russia and England. Kubrick, who rarely shows affection for his characters, presents them with coldness and psychological realism, focusing more on the contexts and invisible forces that shape their destinies.

Set in the period leading up to the French Revolution, the court life, vices, and espionage depicted in *Barry Lyndon* likely represent the deeper causes of European conflicts that Kubrick might have explored in a film about Napoleon. This is especially apparent in the character of Mr. de Balibari, who comes from everywhere and nowhere, and who captivates Barry. Balibari somewhat echoes Veit Harlan's Jud Süß or Shakespeare's Merchant of Venice.

Considering the context of *Barry Lyndon*, Kubrick's study of Napoleon, and his portrayal of World War I in *Paths of Glory*, we can see the central and dominant role that France plays in the globalist architecture as exposed by Kubrick. Through these films, we can trace the occult forces at work in Europe and understand how we arrived at Emmanuel Macron, a modern blend of Napoleon and Alex from *A Clockwork Orange*, a child soldier of the Rothschilds and the satanic global Masonic power, programmed to liquidate everything and carry out a project for global technological dictatorship, with the Olympic Games being a paltry demonstration of this.

Will Macron the swindler face a tragic second act?

The Death of the Father, the Chief Mother, and Tribalism

"Image 1"

"Image 2"

The film *Barry Lyndon* opens with the death of Redmond Barry's father in a duel over a trivial matter concerning the payment for a horse, suggesting a conflict of egos. In the following scene, we see Barry accompanied by his mother, who we learn will remain loyal to her son throughout his life. Symbolically, this scene represents Barry's marriage to his mother, as he never truly has another significant woman in his life.

His mother's influence is always present, providing him with courage during difficult times and fuelling his ambition during good times. She is the driving force behind his desire to attain a noble title, which ultimately leads to his downfall. Cunningly, she instils in him a sense of distrust and tribal instinct.

This tribal instinct is highlighted through Barry's relationships with his own kin. He is deeply infatuated with his cousin, and what might be perceived as homosexual affection for Mr. Balibari, his uncle, and his son is a form of selfishness and tribalism. Barry sees a reflection of himself in Mr. Balibari, particularly in his style and Irish origins. This tribalism prevents Barry from trusting anyone outside his bloodline, further accentuating the impression of psychological imbalance in this otherwise unsympathetic character.

Barry's ambition, fuelled by his mother's influence, drives him to seek a noble title, which becomes his ultimate undoing. His relationships are tainted by selfishness and a narrow focus on his lineage, preventing him from forming genuine connections with others. This selfishness is apparent in his relationships with both men and women, reflecting his deep-seated tribal instincts and distrust of outsiders.

"Image 3"

The final scene of *Barry Lyndon* portrays a destitute and crippled Barry returning to his native countryside, accompanied by his ever-loyal mother. This marks the conclusion of his odyssey. Ultimately, it is she who triumphs, the moribund witch who secures the exclusive company of her son and receives a pension from his ex-wife, Lady Lyndon, either out of pity or in remembrance of the fleeting passion that once sparked their relationship.

This pattern is mirrored in the relationship between Lady Lyndon and her son, Lord Bullingdon, highlighting the tragedy born of human fatality. Barry's nature, overly polarized by ambition and ennui, combined with a thirst for power, renders daily life unbearable and tears families apart. These conflicts stem from the lack of a guiding figure and clear moral compass, which, when absent, lead individuals like Barry to learn life's harsh lessons through experience—often too late.

There is a notable resemblance between Barry Lyndon and the adult Lord Bullingdon, suggesting a perpetuation of the vicious cycle that degrades society and heralds' perpetual conflicts. This cyclical nature is symbolized by the Ouroboros, an infinite cycle that repeats like a shockwave.

In a symmetrical parallel to Barry and his mother, the father and son brigands who rob Redmond at the beginning of his journey are their masculine counterparts. Here, the mother is metaphorically dead instead of the father. Despite their criminality, the brigands show a degree of camaraderie, inviting Barry to share a meal and allowing him to leave without stealing his boots.

"Image 4"

"Image 5"

Barry seems somewhat admiring of the father-son brigands, possibly elevating them to an ideal paternal model. This admiration might influence his future choices and methods. He imagines what his life could have been if his father had lived, envisioning a future where he has a son who resembles him and to whom he will teach the art of brigandry. The young Redmond dreams of conquest and legacy, from his blood and name.

Here, we touch once again on a universal issue: the balance between man and woman and their roles in perpetuating evil through transmission to their children. This cycle of moral and ethical corruption, passed from one generation to the next, underscores the film's exploration of the inherent flaws and tragic destinies of its characters.

The Seven Years' War

The Seven Years' War was the first global conflict, pitting the France-Austria alliance against the England-Prussia alliance and their respective colonial empires in the Americas and India. This war disrupted the relative stability established by the Treaty of Westphalia, which ended the Thirty Years' War in the 17th century. It resulted in a heavy defeat for France and the enduring establishment of the British Empire and the Commonwealth, which persists to this day, directly or indirectly.

At the time, Europe was fragmented, with alliances forming and dissolving based on military strategies, personal networks, egos, and debts. Barry's involvement in these conflicts was highly subjective; he sought personal glory and mere survival. He enlisted out of necessity, joining the English army, which he would desert after the initial battles and the death of his uncle, to reach neutral Holland. Unfortunately, the deserter Barry was captured by a Prussian captain, who gave the young man the opportunity to join his ranks.

Barry developed a certain survival instinct, keeping close to his superiors and away from the thick of the battles. He had a knack for loudly proclaiming his few military exploits, knowing how to varnish his image. Barry navigated the steps necessary for his social advancement with relative ease, demonstrating a talent for building his reputation, particularly through his skill in duelling.

The film pays careful attention to depicting the codes of hierarchical progression within the military organization. As in any human organization, it was more important to please one's master's than to provide quality work or self-sacrifice. Much like in a modern corporation, merit and genius often went unrewarded.

Through a reputation for loyalty built on a moral debt owed by his superior, who owed Barry his life, the end of the Seven Years' War extended into a cold war. Barry was decorated and given a mission to spy on Mr. de Balibary. According to "Barry Lyndon," espionage can be defined as the skill of dining at every table without being caught.

Itinerary of an Opportunist: Fraud, Bluff, and Reputation

"Image 1"

Constancy and dedication are not Barry's strengths. He tends to flee difficulties and is not ashamed to boast of exploits he hasn't achieved. The era is ripe for identity theft and fraud. After all, Barry himself was robbed in his youth. Barry quickly betrays Prussia in favour of the Irish Mr. de Balibari, a gambler and swindler whom he soon greatly admires.

Serving European courts, he enhances his wealth, manners, and cunning by cheating and getting European nobility to sign promissory notes. The hurt egos and debts are settled by duels rather than military conflicts; Barry's duelling skills help preserve their small enterprise's reputation and nobility. The duel becomes a tool for legitimizing the power of the now itinerant croupier.

Barry's rise is never deserved as these steps are haphazard and effortless. His actions are always self-serving, fraudulent, and perverted: such is the case with his relationship with Lady Lyndon—he seduces her effortlessly, and without a word, she falls for him, drawn to his image and varnish.

He then poisons her husband and parasitically takes over his life. Once he secures his position, Barry despises the woman who too quickly gave him what he wanted: a son and a title. Unfortunately for him, his betrayals and frauds do not go unnoticed, and his lack of education and refinement eventually bar him from the nobility he seeks. Barry is a wolf of Wall Street from another era, and the "qualities" that brought him success are the same ones that lead to his downfall.

Usury

Usury, as its name implies, indicates the physical passage of time. A belt becomes worn after months or years, depending on its quality and frequency of use. You might notice stretched holes due to weight gain, which could be adjusted by losing weight or making new holes. A faded colour could be polished, but at a certain level of wear, polish no longer covers the marks of time, and the belt is discarded.

Applied to finance, usury represents the wear and tear on a client from a bank's perspective. The interest rate reflects the use of the client, and varying this rate can regulate the client's burden. Excessive use leads to physical consequences, like pallor, which can be covered with varnish or makeup. When wear becomes too much, another hole is made.

A beautiful buckle, like a noble family crest, can renegotiate terms, often sought by a common belt to maintain the illusion. This logic applies to borrowers, whether individuals or nations: to avoid being replaced like Barry Lyndon, one must tighten the belt and avoid overusing like the plague. The real issue is to always want more.

The Eternal Dissatisfied and Loveless Man

Barry's opportunism and toxic character are rightly sensed by Lord Bullingdon, Lady Lyndon's brave son. At an age when Barry could still have raised him as his own son and shown empathy, he chooses immaturity and disdain, disrespecting his new wife. The father's murder transforms Lord Bullingdon into an effeminate adult driven by vengeance.

The cycle of violence with his stepson is a curse Barry could have avoided, eventually leading to his reputation's destruction and ruin. It's tragic to see a man given everything turn his life into a hell. He indulges in vices, adultery, and alcohol, celebrating his new status like a great conqueror. How can this behaviour be explained? He doesn't understand the value of things and finds joy only within his own tribe. He is miserly with his affection despite his wife's resilience and opportunities for forgiveness. Too attached to his mother's recognition, he cannot act properly, too distrustful to show feelings to a woman he won through cheating and deeply despises.

"Image 1"

"Image 2"

The saying "Ill-gotten gains never prosper" aptly describes Barry's fate. What some may call karma, the Holy Spirit, or immanent justice, eventually finds him, striking his tribe and causing him to lose his titles, his son, and his leg. Barry, who loves only himself and power, under his mother's guidance, undertakes the difficult task of becoming a lord. To gain favor, he pretends to be an art lover, acquiring the "Adoration of the Magi" by the minor painter Cardi, even though he is not a man of the arts. Kubrick would likely have chosen the version by Hieronymus Bosch, as his triptychs, which resemble Kubrick's films, serve as alchemical pictorial initiations of the cosmos, centred on humanity.

Ascending to nobility requires many sacrifices: banquets, courts, invitations, and social abasements are necessary to build a reputation that can collapse in an instant, as it does when Barry publicly confronts his stepson. Indebted, uncultured, and eventually worn out, this fatal error closes the doors of nobility to him. The death of his overly pampered only son, his defeat in the duel with his stepson, his amputation, and his return to his starting point are all punishments for a man who failed to develop sympathy or complicity with his wife.

Despite everything, his wife seems to have a certain gentleness towards Barry; a maternal look that says, "What a shame, Barry. It was up to you to balance the poles, but you wallowed in immaturity."

The nobility worth seeking is first and foremost the nobility of the soul, which allows a man to act as a beacon for his loved ones, mitigate risks, and bring joy despite adversity rather than sadness in opulence. It is less costly. One must still be guided by the heart. Love presents wear and tear.

CHAPITRE 9
Full Metal Jacket

Children? In camps, soldiers they became: a collective fate.
In Vietnam, soldiers and reporters, sharing the same weight:
"To see the foe, just once, a tale to narrate,
Where we're not the villains and enemy is a man"

Co-writer of *Full Metal Jacket*, Michael Herr, a former war correspondent for *Esquire*, said that Kubrick's primary objective was to represent the living, autonomous presence of what Jung calls the Shadow—the most accessible and straightforward human archetype to experience. War and the struggle for power are recurring themes in Kubrick's work. The Vietnam War serves as the backdrop for *Full Metal Jacket*, a film divided into two distinct parts that have become a template for war movies: the first part presents a boot camp, and the second part shows the front-line experience of this group of conscripts, young men turned into war machines.

More than addressing the war itself—since we hardly see a single Viet Cong enemy, except for a woman protecting her family—the film is about ideological indoctrination, brainwashing, and the control of mystique. The objectives are twofold: to make such a war seem legitimate in the eyes of the combatants, thus providing cannon fodder, and to forge history while portraying themselves in a favourable light. This same media cabal, under the control of financial forces, pushes today to present Putin as the aggressor in the Ukraine conflict. Still, its operation is compromised by new technologies and easy access to direct information, which this cabal seeks to censor.

In *Full Metal Jacket*, we witness war from the perspective of a young, innocent, and conscious war journalist who has no choice but to succumb to the dictates imposed by his camp. The choice offered to young men, under the media's pressure, is as follows: the horror of war, as seen through our journalist confronting his shadow, or suicide, as exemplified by the recruit Pyle who refuses to conform.

Kubrick exposes the absurdity of military intervention in Vietnam, the operational functioning of propaganda, the influence of the collective on the individual, and the duality of human nature in the narrative of collective history, explaining all too well the horrors and inhumane atrocities we witness both yesterday and today.

Jordan Peterson, who has spent much of his life questioning the individual mechanisms that drive humans to accept atrocities committed during World War II, would find a synthesis here.

The character of Joker serves as an alter ego of Kubrick, who, under the guise of humour, experiences the darkness of the world with a humanity tinged with cynical despair. Like Joker, Kubrick protested as much as possible while going with the flow of the world.

This is the way.

Equality of Opportunity and Collective Punishment

"Image 1"

The beauty of war is that everyone is equal: black, white, Hispanic, or others, a haircut serves to uniform the individual. Racist jokes abound, yet among these young men, there is no real hostility or jealousy. Like a pack, they assert dominance and strength through testosterone rather than ethnic origin, as shown by the character of Animal Mother, and the only "artificial" racism is that which serves the war, directed at the "yellows." Is racism still a social construct manipulated to divide society and justify wars? Are we still that foolish?

Racial fractures in France and the United States are likely media constructions, strategically emphasized by the need to take sides for or against Israel, aiming to create a clash of civilizations by repeating this conflict in all nations, causing them to collapse from within. But we digress. The power of Satan lies in division; here we have a demonstration, in this form of inter-ethnic fraternity aware of differences but united, that racism does not exist, and that Satan is elsewhere.

While young, enlisted men were once equal, this is no longer the case today thanks to Diversity, Equity, and Inclusion (DEI) policies, which make positive discrimination a mode of operation. These policies encourage the recruitment of women and transgender individuals with more favorable conditions and pay, making sex changes increasingly frequent within Western military organizations. As a result, competence has become secondary, and equal opportunity is a thing of the past. In a perverse manner, we live in a society of identity racism where overly favored minorities overpower the majority. From the perspective of those in power, it's all beneficial: it costs less and causes annoyance. Previously, one had to perform well to advance, now one might have to change their sex. Unfortunately, by continually promoting mediocrity and appearances, it will eventually become apparent, and it already is.

If once enlisted or conscripted young men were equal, this is no longer the case today thanks to Diversity, Equity & Inclusion (DEI) policies, which make positive discrimination a mode of operation. These policies encourage the recruitment of women and transgender individuals with more favourable conditions and pay, having sex changes increasingly frequent within Western military organizations. Thus, competence has become secondary, and equal opportunity a thing of the past. In a perverse manner, we live in a society of identity-based racism where overly favoured minorities overpower the majority. From the perspective of those in power, it's all beneficial: it costs less and causes annoyance. Where previously one had to perform well to advance, now one might have to change their sex. Unfortunately, by continually promoting mediocrity and appearances, it will eventually become apparent, and it already is.

At the camp, Sergeant Hartman, the guardian of troop equality, is there to deconstruct, traumatize, and above all, identify the deviants, the useless, and those who could be a burden to a regiment due to their originality, personality, or inability to submit to the hierarchy. Obedience and meanness are the qualities required of a good soldier; being handy and resourceful are definite advantages, but the media will do the rest: ensuring the hero's image.

Above all, it is doubt and questioning that are unwanted in a soldier, with a sarcastic smile being an expression to be proscribed as it suggests mockery. Mutiny is undesirable, especially mockery of the hierarchy. Without this solid hierarchy, the system wouldn't hold up.

Private Pyle is sarcastic by default; it's hard to know his thoughts, maybe he hides something, or perhaps he can't take this charade seriously, he likely doesn't read newspapers, and doesn't perceive the imminent danger? Or does he have a psychological disorder, a form of autism, or simply deep stupidity? These questions about this inarticulate individual, the black sheep of the camp, remain unanswered for his superiors and comrades, except for Joker, who takes him under his wing like the child he truly is, posing a real risk to the group that needs addressing.

In contrast, Joker is a sarcastic character who doesn't hesitate to provoke his superior, but he is self-assured and opposed to the war. He has the charisma and verbal skills necessary to reassure his troop, the intelligence of an officer to whom men and responsibilities can be entrusted.

The black sheep who jeopardized the regiment becomes the proof of official equal treatment: through collective punishment, everyone is penalized for his mistakes while he eats his donut, the object of the punishment. This practice is notably a form of psychological torture. The entire unit, including his protector Joker, develops a fratricidal hatred for Pyle, which is human nature, and they all become his persecutors first in their opinions of him, then through the savage physical punishment they inflict.

Thus, if Private Pyle is not officially punished as he should be, he is informally punished both physically and spiritually as many times as there are comrades. It is worth noting that to accentuate the psychological and Jungian scope of the film, particularly the duality inherent in human nature and its confrontation with the shadow, the scenes of informal punishments and suicide are filmed at night in a dark, nightmarish luminosity.

This signifies the presence of the autonomous shadow mixed with the collective unconscious, through a compensatory phenomenon of the conscious occurring in dreams at night to restore the balance of the prejudice suffered by the troop during waking hours. At least, that is what Jung would say about dreams—they are a compensatory phenomenon unconscious of conscious reality, in addition to physical restoration. This phenomenon is irresistible, as proven by the participation of the good Joker who takes his turn in the torture, as Pyle himself notes: "Everybody hates me now. Even you."

It is important to understand the spiritual functioning of collective punishment, which has the capacity, as seen here, to drive a person to suicide, making the resolution of humanity's problems extremely delicate. This is especially true in the era of information and control over technologies we have previously discussed, while almost all media are controlled.

Indeed, in a hierarchical society, how can an individual oppose the paying group that holds power? How can a human society, whether a company, an administration, or otherwise, prevent deviant behaviours from those at its top, when at a moment's notice, the paying summit can trigger collective punishment, both physical and psychic, to informally punish the dissident? Is this not the best way to establish a dictatorship and eliminate all resistance? By applying collective punishment, the community itself becomes the system's executioner and punishes the dissidents.

The skills and strength required to resist such pressure are not given to everyone. Who has the strength to face a crowd taken by a delusional frenzy? Jung said it was extremely dangerous to go against the spirit of the times, and he was not wrong, but what can one do when the bad guys have taken control?

For Private Pyle, collective punishment results in the miraculous discovery of his shooting talent. He literally becomes a killing machine and a true legend within the troop (or tribe), which has finally found a useful function for our black sheep. However, the damage is irreversible; his resentment and desire for revenge are expressed in his facial expressions, which are probably also the source for his shooting skills, acquired by visualizing himself shooting bullets into his sergeant's head.

It is apparent that Pyle is ultimately in a psychological conflict, a cognitive dissonance due to his exclusion from a group he vitally needs to be a part of. Collective punishment proves difficult to repair, as he has lost face. It seems that following such punishment, despite a newly constructed reputation, reconstructing karma or relationships with others is difficult, if not impossible, without a change of environment and relationships.

The black sheep identifies two sources of imbalance in his universe, which he seeks to re-balance through a double murder: that of his persecutor, who made everyone aware of his weakness, and his own suicide due to his perception of himself, his now-conscious weakness, and a sense of innate and possibly hereditary injustice.

Through the example of this training camp, we see how an organization like the military formats its recruits and creates its members and executioners through collective punishment.

One can then conceive how a sick head can make a healthy body function or render that body sick.

Vietnam War

"Image 1"

The Vietnam War, often forgotten, was a 20-year conflict that ensnared the United States, marking the first in a long series of defeats. This fratricidal war, conducted on an industrial scale with the massive dumping of napalm and Agent Orange on Vietnamese forests, resulted in 3 million deaths. It pitted Western imperialism against communist nationalism and witnessed the rise of anti-imperialism accompanied by the sexual liberation of youth within the Western bloc as a form of rebellion against a barbaric patriarchal order, weary of an endless war that opened the doors wide to communism, which, as we see now, has changed sides.

In "Full Metal Jacket," the war itself is scarcely shown. The journalist tries in vain to report a victory over the enemy, but there are few enemies in military uniforms. There is a ridiculous attack on their base that takes on circus-like proportions. Most of the casualties are civilians, dead from believing in offers of humanitarian aid or political re-education offered by the US, who are waging a horrible war. This war is primarily ideological, and there is a climate of terror: at the front and the rear, what is wanted is to know the thoughts of one's peers or enemies—you must submit to the ideology or die.

The Viet Cong hide in the forest; they are everywhere and nowhere. Temples and villages are occupied by civilians, women, and children, trampled by young marines seeking a quick victory they will never achieve, themselves victims of a system that completely overwhelms them—drug tests, American industry, and a senseless conflict that places them as invaders while selling them a mission of peace and benevolence.

War scenes are frequently punctuated by interviews; camera crews wander through the rubble and combat scenes; we don't see the enemy, but we praise the quality of the equipment and fighters: this war is an advertisement for the military-industrial complex.

There are some losses; a regiment is routed by snipers. If it is an asymmetric war in terms of means, it is also asymmetric in terms of troop morale, to the disadvantage of the United States, which, with 15 marines against 1 woman, must exert twice the psychological and physical effort to win on this front and keep the propaganda machine running at full speed. The sniper who routes them is a frightened woman, left alone in a ruined building following the bombing of a city, on a suicide mission to prevent the advance of enemy troops.

From the local culture, they take what they can: encounters with cheap prostitutes. They are homesick and see themselves as liberators of an oppressed country, saviours of a South Vietnam incapable of waging its own war. After all, it was probably necessary to prevent the advance of communism, but what was thrown out the door came back in through the window, and the mandrake, the poisoned flower of communism with bureaucracy as its root, as described in "Dr. Strangelove," serves only its own end.

But no matter the ideology as long as there is war, the serpent might say. It's a shame; those temples were quite beautiful.

The Duality of Man and Legitimate Violence

"The desire for privilege and the taste for equality are the dominant and contradictory passions of the French of all times," said de Gaulle.

When Joker is reprimanded by a superior for the contradiction between wearing a peace symbol and his helmet's "Born to Kill" inscription, he responds: "It's about the duality of man, sir—the Jungian thing."

Are we all potential schizophrenics?

Once again, Kubrick's filmography confirms its Jungian inspiration, and this duality is expressed at multiple levels in "Full Metal Jacket." Firstly, the duality of the individual versus the collective, as discussed in the section on collective punishment. Secondly, the duality of the psyche—good versus evil and the necessity of integrating the shadow into the personality. Finally, the masculine/feminine duality previously discussed in the "Eyes Wide Shut" chapter, involving the anima and animus.

These "dualities" are theorized by Jung in his works "Man and His Symbols" and "The Archetypes and the Collective Unconscious."

In the character of Joker, Kubrick expresses a well-integrated model of duality, presenting him as a complete and spiritually superior being: the most human character in the film, probably referencing Colonel Dax from "Paths of Glory." Joker is capable of empathy and patience, an educator and sensitive yet vulnerable to negative emotions, suffering, and anger. These well-integrated aspects allow him courage and intelligent opposition to oppression, embodying a form of legitimate violence.

Joker perfectly personifies the duality of man: his participation in the war contradicts his philosophy because survival instincts and group status drive him—he has no choice. By becoming a war correspondent, he expresses his contradictions, confronts his superiors with humour, and demonstrates his physical and intellectual abilities. He is not affected by cognitive dissonance like

Pyle because he can pay for his mistakes or assume their consequences.

According to Jung, to achieve full personality and psyche development, one must integrate their shadow—the animalistic, instinctive part that drives domination for survival, as theorized in the fight-or-flight response. As the adage goes, "If you want peace, prepare for war," implying that to do good, one must be capable of the worst, while controlling oneself.

Joker demonstrates this during his confrontation with the virile brute Animal Mother, asserting his moral superiority in a verbal joust without losing face. Integrating the shadow allows a person to stand their ground, defend themselves, balance good and evil, and combat evil with legitimate violence.

Joker can deliver the final blow to a wounded Viet Cong woman. By ending her suffering, he commits a morally intrinsic act, or in other words, moral in the eyes of God. They could have tortured her for vengeance or ignored her out of cowardice. In this act of violence, Joker chooses the correct path, demonstrating that legitimate violence is necessary before God. If he couldn't draw his weapon to shoot a woman, risking his life, his deeper spirit whispered the need to end her suffering. Conversely, not committing this act would have been a moral failing—similarly, not resisting obvious oppression is morally reprehensible before God. To resist, one must exhibit legitimate violence: to resist, one must integrate their shadow.

Lastly, note Joker's emphasis on speech against an omnipresent propaganda instrument. Expressing thoughts aloud is an act of active resistance, preserving one's dignity; Joker thus saves his soul. We should all draw inspiration from Joker when, in an administration or organization, as seen during the COVID-19 hysteria, hierarchical and financial pressures push us against our souls to impose inhumane absurdities : speak in accordance with your soul, with politeness and humour.

Self-censorship and collective punishment are the keys to crowd control, turning the world into a forced labour camp. Disobedience and violence are sometimes necessary; find within your soul the balance of poles and remember that truth costs less than the system's lies. The more we tell the truth, the more expensive the lie becomes to them.

Understanding individual duality and its relation to the collective is crucial. Be aware that bad actions, whether conscious through the choice of good or evil or unconscious due to the illusion of good imposed by organizations, ripple through the universe, generally affecting a scapegoat like Private Pyle or resulting in bloodshed in wars compensating for our own weaknesses, at the other end of the world, like in Vietnam or at the borders of Europe, in Ukraine.

Speech, Propaganda, and Western Mystique

Propaganda consists of a set of persuasive techniques implemented to spread an opinion or ideology by all available means. Since speech allows the materialization of reality and can influence the morale of the troops, propagandists have understood that it is speech that must be controlled. Indeed, it seems that reality exists only in the narrative, justifying the use of Newspeak as theorized in "1984," where the meanings of words are completely inverted.

"Image 1"

In the journalists' office, above the sergeant, one can read: "First to Arrive and Last to Know - We Defend to the Death Our Right to Misinform." Kubrick couldn't have been clearer in writing this, gold on red.

The sergeant is visibly eager to end the meeting, and it is noteworthy that Joker is the only one to add fuel to the fire by raising the rumour of a ceasefire suspension. The sergeant dismisses it with the "conspiracy theorist" card and visibly annoyed by the young man's intelligence, must remind him: the role of war journalists is to produce stories that boost troop morale and publish positive stories.

Furthermore, the sergeant is there to control the semantics used in their articles: a "Search and Destroy" operation must be replaced by

"Sweep and Clear"; resistant civilians become soldiers. This classification is crucial in producing statistics and war reporting, as a civilian classified as a military is both one less civilian killed and one more enemy soldier killed.

We are therefore witnessing a war that is primarily mediated, where journalists are the collectors of on-ground information, forced to distort data into dichotomous contortions and reports into euphemisms.

If the military organization has its propaganda and narrative control methods, it's not far-fetched to extrapolate these methods to other public or private sectors, since, in the end, they turn out to be hierarchical organizations uniting human beings with a single goal: divide and conquer.

Whether it's markets, geographical spaces, or available brain time, organizational magic remains the same, and power is exercised in much the same way; thus, a hospital will see its forensic doctors reclassify a post-vaccine death as a COVID death; then technical data analysts will apply filters and transformations, adding two to three additional levels to the data collected by these forensic doctors; then users will apply their filters, under the authority of a boss and a positive storytelling imposed by the organization, just as one can imagine that the news reported to American civilians in the New York Times or New York Post are even more sanitized than those already diluted reported in this office of a US military base in Vietnam.

Through successive informational transformations and thanks to collective and personal punishment (doxing), it is possible to invent a narrative totally at odds with factual reality. This is what Kubrick exposes, revealing the subtle details and the magic of Western mystique through the war propaganda tool that applies to all large human organizations as well as science, as seen in the Lancet Gate, for example.

The true power of Western mystique is in being able to sell one thing while delivering the perfect opposite. We sell peace and deliver war. We sell health and get disease and the opioid crisis. We sell child protection and deliver paedophilia. We sell education and deliver chaos. The source of this mystique lies in organizational structures, power delegations, and control of violence that ultimately directs this mystique, allied with individual weakness that leads everyone to keep their eyes wide shut.

For a society to function, it needs characters like Joker at the top, disinterested in materialism, who have confronted their shadow and possess a moral authority with the means of violence, a moral authority that must be judged and revoked in case of excess.

There must be humans at the top. Without reorganizing organizational structures and powers, in an era of technological omniscience by corrupt actors, partially exposed in "Eyes Wide Shut," the mystique will continue to collapse on itself, dividing people until a widespread late realization, which will probably only be possible in an infamous bloodbath.

From a data analyst's point of view, and I indeed have a bias relative to this function, the core problem to solve, well identified by Kubrick here, in "Dr. Strangelove" and in "Paths of Glory," lies in the gap between procedures, systems, and reporting, which is often a black box attributed to external or internal actors, protecting both their power and the organization's narrative, for a fee.

In this regard, it appears that all data emanating from public or general interest enterprises such as subsidized non-governmental organizations, hospitals, and others should be made public to allow everyone to evaluate and measure performance. Similarly, incident and complaint management systems should be open source and transparent; all reprimands of public matters should be openly visible in public places. Data and statistics available to the average individual are opaque, transformed, and hide a labyrinthine underworld of dark rooms, which we call reporting and systems integration.

As for data collection control, one can rely on the trust of honest agents or on surveillance... provided the surveillance is carried out for virtuous purposes.

Unfortunately, it seems that the mystique is increasingly under the control of a few actors who wish to annihilate any alternative information, as is the case in Australia, France, and the European Union.

We are gradually reaching a crossroads: the end of history through the centralization and totalitarianism of collective mystique à la New York Times, or the advent of a decentralized mystique of community and individual civility.

The decentralization of Western mystique will not happen without a fight and certainly not by restricting our speech.

Within organizations it is more than ever necessary to demonstrate freedom.

CHAPTER 10
Paths of Glory (1957)

As a Gamelin at his desk commands each mission,
While at the frontline, children tread the glorious path wide.
For a franc they execute, they perish, per million's tide,
Yet they may still shed a tear for a German song.

Kubrick's first major studio film, "Paths of Glory," continues his lifelong mission to reveal the mechanisms of global mind control, adding the necessary details to fully understand the system. This film, set during World War I, exposes the hidden power of Freemasonry and its crucial role in global conflicts from the early 20th century in France.

"Paths of Glory" lays bare the technical weaknesses of hierarchical systems and the inhumane treatment of the lower ranks by their superiors in a stunning black-and-white depiction of trench warfare. We will see how, through the establishment of the Republic during the French Revolution, Freemasonry skilfully seized full power in France and has since orchestrated fratricidal conflicts serving the deep state.

The mystique's strength at the time did not allow everyone to analyse the situation correctly or access the information needed to understand it clearly. This old story repeats itself in our era, as demonstrated in previous analyses. Psychological operations (Psy Ops) are not new, and "Paths of Glory" shows their historical roots. The choice of the name "Dax" is significant, pointing again to psychiatry, Scientology, and mind control.

To win, we must tread uncharted paths, think outside the usual framework, persevere, and keep an open mind. The border between the rational and the symbolic will bring the necessary understanding through the intuitive method, as they leave no trace.

France, Freemasonry, and the Gamelins

The French Revolution of 1789 marked the abolition of the old monarchical order, legitimized by the moral authority of the Church, and its gradual replacement by a constitutional and republican organization legitimized by the rights of man and Freemasonry. As former French Education Minister Vincent Peillon put it, Freemasonry is the religion of the Republic.

Adolphe Crémieux, who became Sovereign Grand Commander of the Ancient Scottish Rite and transformed it into the Grand Orient of France, undertook to overhaul the General Regulations of the Rite dating from 1846. Among other proposals, he sought to include the phrase "The Masonic Order's motto is Liberty, Equality, Fraternity..." at the end of Article II. This motto would become the motto of the French Republic in the Constitution of 1848. Adolphe Crémieux was first and foremost a Zionist activist, the grandson of a rabbi, founder of the Alliance Israélite Universelle, who gave his name to the Crémieux Decree granting Algerian Jews French nationality and abolished all discriminatory laws against Jews in France, eventually becoming a lifelong senator of the Third Republic.

One of Napoleon's first major actions during the Revolution was to nationalize hospitals by dissolving the Order of the Hospitallers, which effectively placed hospitals under Masonic control, as were the other organs of state: the military, justice system, and other major administrative and technical bodies.

In this context, France established, through a semblance of democratic regime, full power to Freemasonry, which originated from Jewish Zionist inspiration and inevitably led to moral decadence: moral, political, and military authority became one and the same entity. This is precisely what Kubrick demonstrates in "Paths of Glory."

Indeed, if it can be suspected by his behaviour, the following scene confirms General Broulard's membership in Freemasonry. The pointed finger, the Masonic handshake, the stern look, and his methods of leverage and punishment are all signs of his high rank, and he closely resembles the character of Ziegler in "Eyes Wide Shut."

"Image 1"

"Image 2"

The Gold Room in "The Shining" symbolizes a kind of decision-making cauldron, akin to the French deep state that orchestrates and designs the nation's future without directly involving itself, shielding itself from negative repercussions through insurmountable hierarchical circles, embodying absolute control – the Republic.

This comparison extends to "Eyes Wide Shut" and its ritualistic, tribal orgy: in "Paths of Glory," we witness a ceremony from another era, in a different setting, where mistakes made at the top are paid for at the bottom through officially sanctioned executions disguised as justice.

In the scene where Broulard's dance is interrupted, we observe Lady Broulard's annoyance. Men are here to cater to their wives' desires, highlighting a power dynamic that extends beyond mere political manoeuvring.

The system's operation remains unchanged: protect your masters at all costs. The elite orchestrates from above, making decisions that the lower echelons execute, bearing the brunt of any fallout. This hierarchical protectionism ensures that those at the top remain untouchable, maintaining their power and influence without direct involvement or responsibility for the consequences.

World War I

"Paths of Glory" connects chronologically with "Barry Lyndon," skipping over the Napoleonic period that Kubrick spent years studying. We encounter a society at war, now in a global conflict similar to the one experienced in "Barry Lyndon," but much worse. During the Seven Years' War, battles seemed less violent, and desertion was still a viable option. In trench warfare, retreat is not an option due to the threat of friendly fire; the no man's land, once a site of orderly battles, is now bombarded with mortar fire. A looser hierarchy and organization once allowed room for error, and courage was rewarded rather than punished. Industrial development has also been applied to the military industry, resulting in trench warfare. Soldiers, mired in muddy trenches, struggle to survive or to die quickly. World War I is marked by disfigured faces, disabilities, and injuries: 4,000,000 French soldiers were injured, and soldiers were more worried about returning handicapped than dead, which further demoralized the troops.

The offensive depicted in the film, the capture of a strategic hill named Anthill, and the subsequent execution are inspired by real events. We witness the chain of command leading to the assault: Freemason Major General Broulard orders Freemason Brigadier General Mireau, who then orders non-initiate Colonel Dax to launch an immediate attack on the target without any additional resources. It is implied that Broulard is granting a favor to someone within his network, a network to which Mireau and Dax do not have access. Despite his fears, Dax agrees to the assault, which predictably ends in failure.

World War I changed the scale of warfare, resulting in millions of casualties. It became a war of numbers and conscription to face heavy artillery, reminiscent of the current war in Ukraine against Russia: a suicidal high command with objectives that have little to do with the state's victory over the enemy. Instead, we should look for reasons rooted in industry and the interests of transnational bureaucrats. Indeed, who benefits from the crime? Never retreating seems to be a condition of bluffing, wearing down the opponent by forcing them to massacre their own troops to inflict a media defeat on them.

World War I saw two major and lasting changes: the Balfour Declaration to the Rothschild family, recognizing a state of Israel in Palestine, and the Trotsky-inspired Bolshevik Revolution in a floundering Russia, which then withdrew from the conflict.

We see how, by whom, and for whom the power of the French high command is exercised. It only takes connecting the dots.

Note-Taking, Official Reports, and Abuse of Power

To accentuate points raised earlier, especially in the analysis of "Full Metal Jacket," and to highlight Kubrick's meticulous attention to bureaucratic details where the devil subtly hides, let's delve into the three different cases mentioned in "Paths of Glory."

Case 1: Lieutenant Roger's Report

The first case involves the drafting of the report by Lt. Roger, who, while intoxicated, killed a team member with a grenade during a reconnaissance mission. Upon returning to the trench, he is required to write the mission report as per usual procedure. It becomes apparent that he has complete control over the survivor, as he can write anything he wants in the report without any witnesses other than the sole survivor. He could easily make false accusations and hold the survivor responsible for his own error. Here, we see another demonstration of the weaknesses of bureaucracy and the exercise of power. This logic can be easily transposed to the civilian world, such as in the notes and reports written daily by caregivers in a psychiatric hospital about an interned patient who has no access to the collected data and no real option to challenge the caregivers' reports.

Case 2: General Mireau's Order

The second case involves General Mireau's order to bombard his own retreating troops. Operator Rousseau refuses the order without a written proof signed by the General himself, who then issues threats of demotion, revealing an obvious attempt at abuse of power by Mireau. Rousseau, well-versed in the regulations, successfully thwarts this attempt. Mireau refuses to sign such an order, which would be a perfect proof of his responsibility. This detail is crucial as it demonstrates how some managers, section chiefs, and hierarchies operate to absolve themselves of responsibility by making unofficial requests under official guises and benefiting from others' errors. Another method is to place the responsibility for a decision on a newcomer, an absentee, or someone on sick leave, such as burnout. Imagine the behavior of a boss towards an employee if the employee is compromised in any way. This shows how wars and poor political decisions are orchestrated: no one is responsible, yet everyone is. Thus, we end up with a ghost pirate ship at the helm of the world's greatest military power, as is the case with Joe Biden's United States.

Case 3: The Mock Trial

The final type of abuse of power is the mock trial of the three men selected for the court-martial. Colonel Dax repeatedly notes that there are no official notes taken and that the charges other than cowardice before the enemy are not stated. It becomes clear that all authority emanates from the same top, and the decision is made before the trial takes place, as must often be the case in a Masonic republic. We witness the practical demonstration of the exercise of totalitarian power within a supposed democracy where a court-martial is merely an administrative formality to validate the procedure according to the constitution, stage a defense, and provide the media with the image of justice.

These three cases are excellent examples of how unwritten law operates within human organizations and how human nature, tribalism, speech, power, and evil often prevail over procedures, written law, and the common good.

Law, Charisma, and Power

The law is written for those without power. Power, as shown in "Eyes Wide Shut," is determined by rank within the dominant sect. Charisma, on the other hand, is an individual trait related to personality and experience that allows one to apply unwritten laws and seize power through intellectual and moral dominance within a codified environment. In the Church, it is said that priests develop charisma, aura, and reputation during their priesthood. The charisms of the Church include the charisma of speech, discernment, and healing, also known as "spiritual gifts." This charisma, this reputation, helps make them unquestionable authorities within a given environment.

Charisma allows for the substitution of written laws, for instance, by erecting a mock justice to enforce unwritten laws instead of the written ones. The written laws emanate from the dominant sect and tacitly state that someone, somewhere, must pay for the mistakes committed, regardless of their actual responsibility, to maintain balance in the universe and atone for faults.

General Mireau possesses a warrior charisma, symbolized and accentuated by the scar on his cheek, showcasing his experience with violence. General Broulard, on the other hand, seems to have an altruistic charisma and recognizes a similar trait in Colonel Dax—courageous and just leadership. Broulard assigns the dirty work to Mireau and claims the image of a just figure by allowing the court martial. This decision enhances his charismatic and media presence, while Mireau's martial charisma is exacerbated and used against him, making him a (legitimate) scapegoat for the violence of war.

Power operates on rational selfishness: the pursuit of power is an end in itself. When Dax seeks to defend his men using bureaucratic leverage, Broulard recognizes his political competence and ambition to join the decision-makers' table. He sees in Dax a new knight whose charisma is more useful than his bishop (Mireau) on the political chessboard. Dax's altruistic charisma is superior to Mireau's. For Broulard, altruism is merely charisma and veneer to achieve his ends. When he recognizes Dax's honest heart, he rejects and sends him to his death. However, Dax seems protected by the gods, as evidenced by his venture into no man's land and his safe return.

This example shows how deep power uses personal charisma to serve an end: the end justifies the means. From the perspective of power—whether religious, political, military, or administrative—the development of an individual's charisma serves only one end: to gain personal power. Therefore, in the public sphere, charisma is the political facade, which is the art of acquiring and retaining power.

Understanding this, we see the importance of counterpowers and legitimate violence against tyrannical regimes, and why American Democrats are so keen to modify the Second Amendment. In France, citizens seemingly can only endure tyranny without any means of defense, as was the case for the heavily repressed yellow vests.

An anomaly in the power structure, clearly highlighted in "Paths of Glory," is self-sacrifice. Generalizing self-sacrifice within a hierarchical chain can undermine the entire structure. This is evident in Broulard's reaction when Dax proposes to take his men's place at the court martial. Lifetime contracts, unemployment systems (in France), and debt are elements that make self-sacrifice rare in human organizations, which generally tend to offload their problems onto others.

Power defends itself well but governs poorly, seeing self-sacrifice as the ultimate folly. Unfortunately, there will be no change without self-sacrifice.

The Prison Chaplain

The prison chaplaincy is a long-standing French tradition, with Vincent de Paul being the first priest appointed as chaplain of the galleys by the king. This Christian tradition is based on the Gospel imperative: "I was in prison, and you came to visit me!" From this, a rich Christian tradition of visiting prisons has developed.

One could cite Jean Rodhain as the most illustrious prison chaplain in France. Appointed by de Gaulle in 1946, he was the founder of Secours Catholique and Caritas Internationalis. This interesting figure understood the power of words and the importance of mystique. He famously said, "If I had to choose between a check and a microphone, I would choose the microphone. For truth is the first charity." Jean Rodhain was a brilliant priest, a being of light who saw Hollywood as an example to follow for transmitting God's message and amplifying his actions.

In a secular French Republic, the lower echelons of society retain a strong Catholic identity, and the charisma of the priest is used by the system to deliver bad news, lubricate and legitimize judicial decisions, while providing a semblance of counterpower and morality. The priest gives blessings and takes confessions before executions, and likely does his best to mend the breaches of power, such as with families, by correcting explanatory letters and messages.

The limited and peripheral power of this religious organization is not new, and it appears that religious organizations are all infiltrated by the globalist sect. It should not be forgotten that the Church is yet another organizational matrix with bureaucratic functioning, vulnerable to the mandrake, and often tainted by sordid stories. Is everything to be discarded?

Nothing should be discarded except the Pope's authority: the Church should be a decentralized organization. We must remember the fate that the Catholic organization offered to the Cathars, who were professionals in self-sacrifice and material disinterest, imitating the model of Christ: they were all massacred.

The Cathars, through their disinterest in material wealth and hierarchy, threatened all mechanisms of control. Everything points to this conclusion. Their existence and practices put them at odds with the control mechanisms of the established Church, leading to their ultimate persecution and eradication.

Colonel Dax and Psychiatrist Cunningham Dax

In the character of Colonel Dax, we see the archetype of a good man. Here, another strange coincidence presents itself: the psychiatrist Cunningham Dax, perfectly aligning with our central theme.

Dr. Dax was an English psychiatrist who spent most of his career in Australia. Dax was a colleague of John Rawlings Rees, a psychiatrist in the Royal Navy and a Scottish member of the Methodist Church. It's worth noting that during World War II, Rees oversaw the detention of Rudolf Hess, a high-ranking German officer who had attempted to prevent the UK from entering the war by flying solo to meet the Duke of Hamilton, only to be imprisoned by MI5. Hess was subsequently kept alone in Spandau Prison, a facility designed for 800 inmates, until his death in 1987. His diaries accused Colonel Rees of attempting to poison, drug, and hypnotize him. Hess was found dead, purportedly a suicide, and his gravestone bore the inscription: "I dared."

Returning to Dax, if he was trained in lobotomies and electroshock therapy by Rees, he was also an innovator. In 1953, he published a study on psychiatric treatment through art therapy and collected artworks created by his patients. The Cunningham Dax Collection has become one of the largest of its kind in the world.

Shortly after the release of *Paths of Glory*, Dr. Dax was attacked by the Australian Church of Scientology for his physical treatment methods. It should be noted that Scientology in Australia was exposed in the Anderson Report for wanting to use Australia as a "platform to take control of the entire world." Scientology has always used the "electro psychometer" to measure emotional reactions through the body's electrical frequencies.

From 1969 to 1978, Dax was the coordinator of community health services within the Mental Health Services Commission in Tasmania. Dr. Dax later returned to Victoria but continued to provide diagnoses and recommendations for Tasmanian patients, including Martin Bryant in 1984, who committed the Port Arthur massacre in 1996. This event led to a large-scale campaign for gun control and regulation across Australia. Bryant had likely been programmed, having inherited a house and a large sum of money from a deceased partner who was probably part of the network. This enabled him to travel extensively before embarking on his deadly rampage. Gun control is a crucial step in establishing a global dictatorship by the deep state, creating a monopoly on violence.

This coincidence links Scientology, event fabrication, and the articles in *Eyes Wide Shut*. What can be deduced? It seems that Scientology serves as a useful idiot for the global domination system. By criticizing and attacking traditional psychiatric treatments, they serve the globalist sect. Did they want to blame Dr. Dax for the Port Arthur attacks? The truth is murky, but this event checks all the boxes of a "fabricated event," whether it originated from Scientology or traditional psychiatric treatment systems.

Perhaps Kubrick, by presenting Dax as the good man, wanted to point us towards a third path: neither chemical, electrical, nor satanic, but psychiatric treatment through artistic expression.

A German Song

In the final scene, we see Colonel Dax approaching a tavern, his men drinking and shouting at a German woman, played by Kubrick's future wife, Christiane Harlan. Disillusioned with his superiors, Dax is struck by vertigo: Is there no hope for humanity? Is man a mere animal, and is civilization doomed? Then the pretty blonde begins to sing timidly in German, and everyone starts to hum along and weep.

This scene is the most emotional in Kubrick's entire filmography. Man is not a beast because beauty is universally recognized in the vibrations of the earth; he becomes a beast when beauty disappears.

CHAPTER 11
Deus Ex Machina

Through his films, Stanley Kubrick consistently warns against various societal dangers: tribalism, hierarchy, the food and military industries, technology, and Freemasonry. He symbolically expresses his concern about the overwhelming power of those who control the mystique through media event fabrication and who attempt to suppress the benefits of technology for the greater good. Kubrick's films suggest that while God may be a machine, as described in *Eyes Wide Shut*, this machine is already operational. According to *2001: A Space Odyssey*, the real problem lies in the programming of this machine for the subjugation of humanity by one tribe over others, rather than in the technology itself.

In this section, we will explore DARPA (Defense Advanced Research Projects Agency), its operations, key actors, and its connections to the CIA and major universities. We will also discuss the emergence of "targeted individuals," a phenomenon highlighted by the Havana Syndrome.

DARPA was created in 1958 in response to the Soviet Union's launch of Sputnik. Its mission is to make pivotal investments in breakthrough technologies for national security. Over the decades, DARPA has been involved in numerous projects that have significantly advanced technology, including the development of the internet, stealth technology, and precision-guided munitions.

DARPA operates closely with the CIA and collaborates with leading universities to advance its research goals. This relationship facilitates the rapid development and deployment of new technologies. Universities provide a fertile ground for research, while the CIA offers operational expertise and security clearances necessary for sensitive projects.

The phenomenon of "targeted individuals" has become more prominent in recent years, with the Havana Syndrome being the most widely recognized example.

The Havana Syndrome refers to a set of medical symptoms reported by U.S. and Canadian embassy staff in Havana, Cuba, starting in late 2016. Symptoms include hearing strange grating noises, ear pain, vertigo, and nausea. While the exact cause remains unknown, some theories suggest the involvement of directed energy weapons.

Targeted individuals claim to be victims of covert harassment and surveillance, often involving electronic weapons and psychological warfare. These claims, though controversial and often dismissed by authorities, highlight the potential misuse of advanced technologies developed by agencies like DARPA.

The case of James Tilly Matthews, an 18th-century British merchant, and political activist, provides a historical example of the use of psychiatric control over dissidents. Matthews claimed to be targeted by a machine he called the "Air Loom," which he described as a complex device operated by a gang of criminals. They supposedly used this machine to influence his thoughts and actions through "magnetic fluids." While his claims were dismissed as delusional, Matthews' case illustrates early concerns about technological control over individuals.

Matthews' story underscores the complicity and corruption within the psychiatric field. Historically and today, psychiatry can be used to discredit and control serious dissidents. This method of engendering madness among troublesome free spirits persists, as seen in modern cases like Matthew Choi.

DARPA, the BRAIN Initiative, and IBM

In this section, we will explore the risks posed by organizations like DARPA and their advanced technologies, which may have fallen into the hands of criminal elements, reinforcing our analysis of Kubrick's filmography. It is important to note that the following analysis is based on sources available before the COVID-19 pandemic, and the trend has likely intensified since then.

DARPA (Defense Advanced Research Projects Agency) is a U.S. agency tasked with developing new warfare technologies, maintaining the technological superiority of the U.S. armed forces, and preventing technological advancements by its adversaries. It is the most powerful, secretive, and well-funded military scientific agency globally. Created by the U.S. Congress in 1958, DARPA receives an annual budget of approximately $3 billion. The agency does not conduct its own scientific research but contracts defence contractors, academics, and other governmental organizations to perform the work, then facilitates the application of the results for military use. This makes DARPA a central figure in global mind control.

DARPA maintains a minimal staff, averaging 120 program managers annually. U.S. higher education institutions and university research centres have been the crucibles where many of DARPA's innovations have been developed.

Among the weapons the United States is developing are mind control weapons. These highly secret DARPA projects are likely linked to high-risk human experimentation involving various criminal organizations, hospitals, and intelligence services. Recent research suggests that several DARPA-related mind control projects are currently being developed in Latin America and Africa, involving illegal human experimentation.

Citizens may be intoxicated with beverages and foods contaminated with nanoparticles and brain nanorobots and kidnapped to install brain implants, such as cortical modems or artificial hippocampi, without their consent.

The BRAIN Initiative (Brain Research through Advancing Innovative Neurotechnologies) is a collaborative effort launched by the U.S. government in 2013 to accelerate the development and application of innovative technologies to map the brain's circuitry, understand how the brain works, and uncover ways to treat, prevent, and cure brain disorders. DARPA is one of the key players in this initiative, along with other organizations like the National Institutes of Health (NIH) and the National Science Foundation (NSF).

While the BRAIN Initiative aims to advance our understanding of the brain and develop new treatments for neurological diseases, there are concerns about the potential misuse of these technologies for mind control and surveillance.

IBM has been a significant player in developing advanced computing technologies, including artificial intelligence (AI) and quantum computing. These technologies have the potential to revolutionize various fields, from healthcare to cybersecurity. However, they also pose significant risks if used unethically.

IBM's involvement in AI research, particularly through its Watson AI system, has raised concerns about data privacy and the ethical implications of AI decision-making. The integration of AI with brain-computer interfaces (BCIs) and other neurotechnologies being developed under the BRAIN Initiative could lead to unprecedented levels of surveillance and control over individuals.

The BRAIN Initiative was launched in 2013 by then-President Barack Obama in the United States, Australia, and several other countries to unify efforts in developing global mind control technologies. A Netflix film released in 2022, "Leave the World Behind," produced by Obama, highlights these technologies and indicates a movement towards their official recognition. Similarly, the film "Les Survivantes" by Barnerias, featuring Hélène Pelosse, a former minister and UN representative, who testifies to microwave attacks and threats against her children, underscores these concerns. I, too, have been a victim of these attacks, which I will detail in the second volume of my work.

DARPA has invested over $500 million to support the White House's BRAIN Initiative. The risks associated with researching these technologies have led to unauthorized experimentation on non-volunteers, often involving so-called "nano-mafias." These projects, which utilize nanorobots, share a common model: they are developed through telemetry, via Wi-Fi, lacking physical form and being intangible. This "nano-mafia" is essentially a Wi-Fi mafia, an almost impossible-to-identify ghost mafia. As Kubrick's films suggest, DARPA and the security nano-mafia have laid the groundwork for a global cerebral internet network, leveraging universities and broadcasting hardware for radio, television, and telephone transmission.

For instance, Jo-An Occhipinti, director of the Brain and Mind Centre at the University of Sydney, is married to a global radio and broadcasting security engineer from global security company Irdeto. This type of tribal arrangement is found in all countries, where physical broadcasting networks are closely intertwined with Brain Initiatives and the psychiatry departments of renowned universities.

Consequently, what you watch, listen to, and eat can be monitored, and necessary suggestions can be made to influence your actions and remotely control you. This goes beyond mere suggestion; they have a complete technological mix that allows them to control one or multiple individuals remotely. It is highly likely that the attempted assassination of Trump was a significant technical demonstration of this capability.

Below is a recent list of participants from an African Brain Initiative conference, with Professor Harris Eyre, a descendant of a powerful Royal Navy family, being a central figure: Professor Harris Eyre - A prominent figure in the BRAIN Initiative, Eyre comes from a distinguished Royal Navy family.

IBM, identified by Kubrick as a frontrunner in advanced technologies, is considered one of the principal partners of DARPA, which funds most of its neuroscientific projects. Remember that Ferdinand Freudenstein from Columbia University and Stanford offered his services to IBM, and his dynasty extends to Australia, influencing media (NewsCorp, Foxtel) and social services (Uniting). The extract from the Art Gallery of NSW serves as a reminder of the Woke dictatorship this network aims to establish.

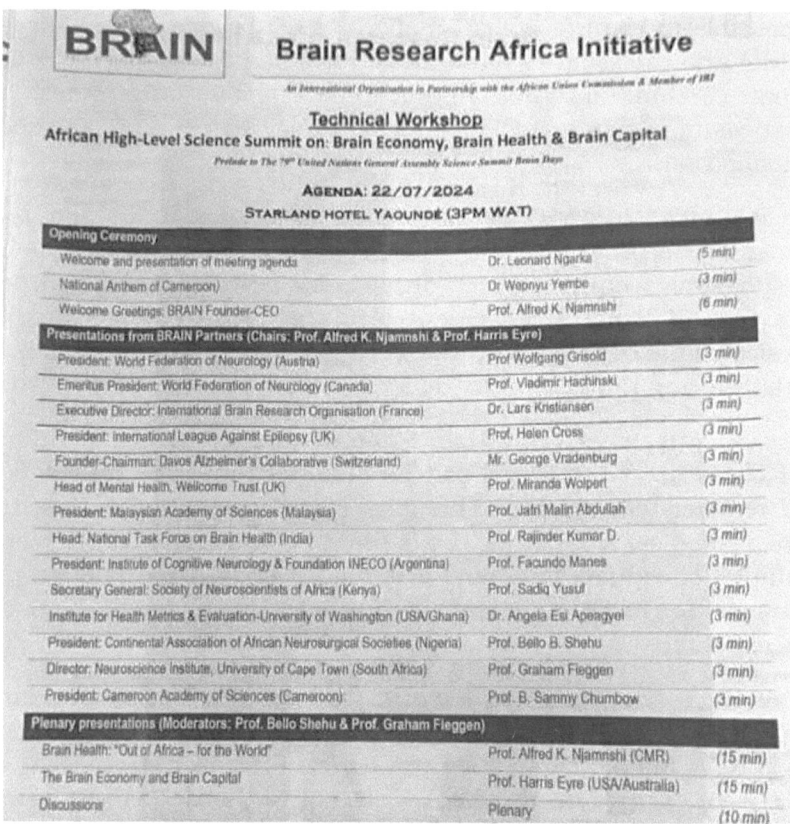

Public Agenda from Brain Initiative Africa

A 2019 article by Dr. Flores points to IBM conducting illegal human experimentation through its hospital, university, and mafia networks to achieve "brain mapping" in Mexico and Peru, where Silicon Valleys of Latin America have emerged. The unsettling truth is that since the global rollout of mRNA vaccinations, we are already within a global network of "sentient AI" or sensitive artificial intelligence that scans and evaluates all your interactions, possibly using the measurement and analysis of the Cosmic Microwave Background (CMB), enabling remote human control akin to operating a machine. These technologies are likely under the control of mafias and private or semi-private security groups, including IBM and DARPA, who program this technology for their own benefit.

Cognitive Warfare, Freedom Fighters and Targeted Individuals

We have entered the era of cognitive warfare, a term that is comprehensively discussed in the 2023-2024 NATO Military Technology Trends report. This report highlights a wide array of new technologies available for warfare, which in reality, are already in use today. There is no public debate on this topic, with the only notable public figure addressing it being the Israeli globalist alarmist Yuval Noah Harari, who is also entangled in these networks.

I encourage you to conduct a Google search for "targeted individuals" to find numerous testimonies that echo the experiences of James Tilly Matthews. The deep state, controlling military hierarchies and technologies that may have fallen into the hands of mafias, is deploying its arsenal against free dissidents, often using them as subjects for large-scale testing.

This hypothesis was confirmed on May 8, 2024, by the U.S. Internal Security Committee, where CIA representatives admitted to using mind control technologies on their own citizens during the Havana Syndrome investigation. This is yet another partial truth that conceals the full extent of the deep state's enterprise and the range of available technologies.

Besides previous organisations, SERCO, a civilian and military contractor, is one of the primary actors in global mind control and has significant influence in most Western governments. This organization has the means to inflict suffering and is involved in numerous scandals, even being referenced in Kubrick's "The Shining." Understanding the existence and operation of these technologies is the first necessary step to regulate and prevent the abuses of this technological and administrative mix.

A perfect example of a free dissident who has suffered organized attacks by the deep state is the young programmer named Matthew Choi. Persecuted by authorities in South Africa and then in Hong Kong, Choi endured escalating attacks and eventually killed a taxi driver following the publication of explanatory videos on the sentient AI system on YouTube. Controlled and influenced by this technology,

Choi was led to commit the murder, resulting in his incarceration at the high-security Siu Lam prison, where he is currently awaiting trial.

Choi had arrived at the same conclusions as I have, possibly too early: the deep state controls a radio-orchestrated technology, semi-independently managed by a Human-in-the-Loop AI. Proving that Matthew Choi was a victim of this technology and identified as a free dissident during his act could help recognize the use of these weapons and raise awareness about these methods. I call on international lawyers interested in the subject to take up this case.

There is a pressing need to launch a serious international defence movement to recognize, identify, and defend against these attacks, as well as to combat the power of the deep state and psychiatric networks. This movement should aim to:

Develop Counter Technologies

Develop an AI system capable of balancing existing system in place. It is likely that Grok from Elon Musk will play this role.

Raise Awareness

Educate the public and policymakers about the existence and dangers of cognitive warfare technologies. Disseminate information on the testimonies of targeted individuals and the historical context of such technologies.

Legal Defense

Provide legal support to victims like Matthew Choi. Advocate for international laws regulating the use of mind control technologies and protecting citizens from such abuses.

Research and Documentation

Conduct independent research to document cases of targeted individuals and the use of cognitive warfare.Collaborate with experts in neuroscience, technology, and human rights to create comprehensive reports.

Policy Advocacy

Lobby for the implementation of stringent regulations on the development and use of cognitive warfare technologies. Work with international bodies to establish oversight mechanisms and accountability for the use of such technologies.

The Air-Loom Machine and James Tilly Matthews: patient zero of cognitive warfare?

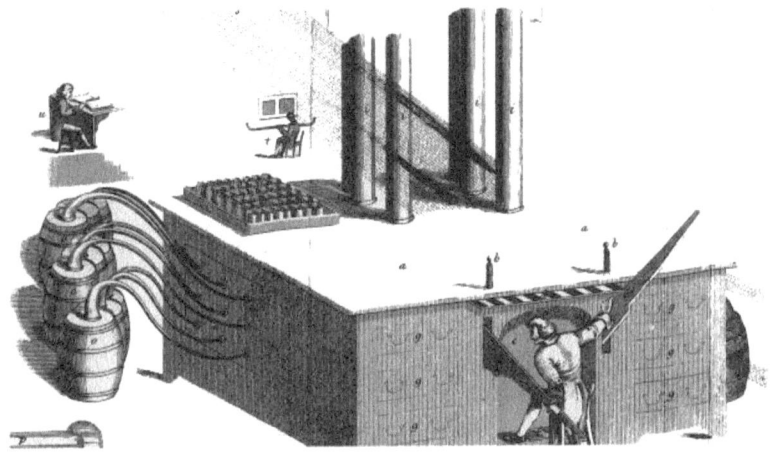

Technical drawing of the Air Loom Machine by James Tilly Matthews 1809, Public domain

In the technical drawing we see here, James Tilly Matthews depicted the terrifying machine he called the "Air-Loom." Matthews, a Franco-English spy and peace activist during the Napoleonic Wars, was confined to Bedlam Asylum in London in 1797. He believed that his mind was under the control of this horrific machine, whose mesmeric rays and mysterious gases were brainwashing politicians and plunging Europe into revolution, terror, and war. Mike Jay tells the story in his book, *The Influencing Machine: James Tilly Matthews and the Air Loom*, which I highly recommend understanding the workings of the Anglo-Saxon psychiatric system and its political uses, which have not changed since.

The Air-Loom operated by weaving gases in a "magnetic fluid field" which was then directed at its victim. Matthews' explanation of these powers combined the cutting-edge technologies of pneumatic chemistry and the electric battery with Mesmer's controversial science of animal magnetism. The details grow increasingly bizarre: the machine was powered by combinations of fetid effluvia, including "spermatic-animal-seminal rays" and "putrid human breaths." Its magnetic field attacked Matthews' brain, and the ultimate goal of this mind control system was the "forging of events," i.e., controlling key actors and events to steer history in a certain direction and execute a Machiavellian plan of control.

These techniques included "brain-saying" (suggestion of ideas) and "dream-working" (implantation of dreams), through which thoughts were imposed on him against his will. There was also a terrifying array of physical tortures, from joint pain and tearing of vital organs to the dreaded "nutcracker," where the air around his chest was tightened until he could no longer breathe. He was relentlessly tormented by hallucinations, physical pain, bouts of laughter, and being forced to repeat what others chose for him to say. It is unsurprising that some people thought he was mad.

According to Matthews, the operators of the machine were a band of infiltrated Jacobin terrorists, whom he described with striking precision. Their goal was the forging of events. Their leader, Bill the King, was a faceless, merciless blackmailer known "never to smile"; his second-in-command, Jack the Schoolmaster, carefully took notes on the operations of the Air-Loom. The operator was a dark woman covered in scars, known only as "The Glove Woman." The public face of the gang was a sharp-faced woman named Augusta, superficially charming and charismatic but "execrably evil and cunning," who roamed the West End of London as an infiltrated agent.

Matthews' story, while seemingly outlandish, highlights the intersection of technology, psychology, and political manipulation. His experiences can be seen as an early precursor to modern concerns about mind control, surveillance, and psychological warfare. The concept of the Air-Loom machine echoes in today's discussions about advanced neurotechnologies, brain-computer interfaces, and the potential for abuse in the hands of powerful entities.

As we enter the era of cognitive warfare, the parallels between Matthews' Air-Loom and current technologies used for influence and control become evident. DARPA's Brain Initiative, IBM's neuroscientific experiments, and the global reach of intelligence agencies all suggest a sophisticated and pervasive system of control that echoes the fears and experiences of Matthews. The narratives of "targeted individuals" today reflect similar experiences of manipulation and torture, albeit with more advanced technologies.

James Tilly Matthews is often cited as the first clinical case of paranoid schizophrenia and psychosis, particularly for his belief in the "influencing machine": the idea that a device operated secretly from afar could control his mind and body. But could it be that Matthews uncovered a hidden truth? Could his "band of event forgers" be the ancestors of modern intelligence agencies like the CIA and MI5, as well as Masonic lodges? Could the putrid effluvia Matthews described be the predecessors of today's chemical agents used in the food industry, which increase the suggestibility of targets, with modern suggestion techniques enhanced by televisions, radios, phones, and satellites?

James Tilly Matthews might well be seen as patient zero, or the first guinea pig, especially given his transnational ties between France and England during the pivotal period of the French Revolution. His "band of event forgers" could be likened to the modern-day group of chemist-hypnotists at the Ziegler House in Kubrick's films. Dr. Carleton Simon, with his combination of expertise in chemistry, psychiatry, law enforcement, and propaganda, fits the profile of a master manipulator leading a team of chemists and polar explorers.

If we consider that all Western governments, under the control of this group, have subjugated the police, social services, psychiatry, and scientific communities, and that anyone claiming to have been poisoned or exposed to such a machine is immediately deemed insane and institutionalized, we face a daunting reality. This is evident in the dismissive Wikipedia article on electromagnetic harassment, which begins, "Electromagnetic harassment is a conspiracy theory [...]".

Are we dealing with an invisible, indefensible weapon that has been shaping events and narratives for over 200 years? Is the Air-Loom machine the prototype of generalized modern cognitive warfare? Proving this deception could challenge the legitimacy of the French Revolution itself, suggesting it was influenced by early chemical weapons.

What does this mean for human rights, and how can individuals engage with this mystique? If God is indeed a machine, then it falls upon us to take responsibility for its programming. The implications are profound: we must ensure transparency and accountability in the development and application of these technologies to safeguard individual freedoms and truly democratic processes.

CHAPTER 12
Heirloom and Opening

Heirloom

The Loom of Invisible Strings and Foul Breath
Animates souls with unseen flow,
Induces actions to vulnerable beings,
Cleans its tracks and erases the Fighters.

All-seeing, increasingly, by the grace of processors,
Its knowledge, family jewel of predecessors,
"Heritage" in French, passed down,
Tortures and dirty words to children.

Ammonia and sodium, the paranoid opiums,
Mixed by voodoo with amino acids,
Weave threads, suggested symbols,
To the puppet frightened by its celiac disease.

What if a better-prepared spy, in his guts,
A Girondin for peace, James Tilly Matthews,
Ambidextrous and lucid, attempted to defuse
The "Air-Loom" encoded; schizophrenia diagnosed.

And long the years to rehabilitate his name and prove his essence!
Maybe two or three familiar friends to deny his madness,
Meditations, fasts, perseverance, and words, and science,
His true allies against the strange fractal, machine of Life.

*Héritage en anglais

If the situation is alarming and the game seems lost, the world is in a constant power struggle, and it is evident that antagonistic forces are fighting for control of these technologies. The only way, as shown in 2001, is to fight against it with it.

In this section, we will ask ourselves how we can face this and regain control of our destiny. The most important step has already been taken for you: becoming aware of it.

For the rest, we will have many things to do.

Controlling Psychiatric Services

As demonstrated in our analysis of A Clockwork Orange, the psychiatric sector plays a key role in exercising power against dissidents, particularly through the diagnosis of schizophrenia, which covers a broad range of symptoms.

To exercise citizen control over psychiatric hospitals, it is necessary to develop a custom or practice that allows anyone to visit psychiatric patients locally and regularly, much like a prison chaplain. This would offer moral support and act as a counterbalance to the overarching power of the psychiatric system. Simply walking through a psychiatric hospital could already help monitor and prevent abusive practices. This practice should be permitted in all publicly funded organizations.

Furthermore, the over-prescription of medications, while beneficial to pharmaceutical companies, is detrimental to the community, as antipsychotic drugs produce irreversible negative effects.

Consent to treatment in these institutions is never free and informed; it is constrained. It is necessary to turn these opaque services into public interest organizations in which citizens can freely participate. It is also essential to increase the possibilities for external contact, whether by phone or face-to-face, and allow patients easy access to external food deliveries of their choice, as opposed to being restricted to company-run canteens like Sodexo.

Nutrition, Fasting, and Self-Sufficient Food Production

One of the key elements to retain from Kubrick's filmography is the food vector of the deep state. If our analysis is correct, companies like Coca-Cola, the United Nations, and all large-scale industrial food production groups such as SYSCO, Unilever, Sodexo, and water treatment organizations, are vying for the right to magnetize their customers.

In France, due to corrupted governmental organizations like SAFER, which sell the country to the highest bidders, notably China, we have lost our food autonomy, and farmers are being expropriated through administrative hazing. We have become dependent on the food and chemical industry, which aims to enslave and control our minds. Here are some ways to break free from this control:

Complete Water Fasting: To regain self-control, complete water fasting is an effective countermeasure against negative vibrations and psychic attacks that may be inflicted on you. By fasting for periods of 3 to 10 days for healthy individuals, we can demagnetize ourselves and realign our bodies to healthy vibratory frequencies.
The oligarchy detests fasting because it restores self-control to the individual. Fasting is a spiritual sacrifice that has the potential, if performed on a national scale, to temporarily break the magnetic hold. Reading *Fasting Can Save Your Life* by Herbert Shelton is recommended to understand all aspects of fasting.

Avoid Industrial Products: Avoid all industrial products, fluoride (which calcifies the pineal gland), sugar, alcohols, MSG, and flavour enhancers, as well as all company canteens. Instead, prioritize products whose origin and production methods you know.

Self-Produce as Much as Possible: Produce as many of your own food products as you can and control the production methods by directly informing yourself about the products and seeds used, by directly contacting farmers.

Take Control of Reporting and Data

1. Step Away from Smartphones: The first action to take is to distance yourself from smartphones. Stop giving the machine the keys to your personal program.

2. The Reality Behind the Screens: On the screens, everything seems fine, but on the ground, everything is going wrong. As shown in *Paths of Glory* and *Full Metal Jacket*, the function of reporting is crucial in decision-making and maintaining state lies. This function must return to the citizens.

3. Transparency in Government and NGOs: Governments increasingly outsource their services to private agents, associations, and NGOs, which hold negotiation power and leverage over the paying governments. These organizations operate with deliberately opaque reporting, making it impossible to track results and the effective use of public funds. The same goes for international organizations that directly impact nations: WHO, UN, NATO, WEF. To understand their decisions, we must demand full disclosure of their decision-making mechanics.

4. Accountability in Public Spending: These entities, which act as public fund siphons, drain the soul of nations with minimal results and extensive control: hospitals, disability organizations, social services, etc., have become lucrative new businesses for key players who are hard to identify. This phenomenon has accelerated since the COVID-19 episode, lockdowns, and the democratization of remote work.

5. Verification of Scientific Publications: We can no longer accept scientific publications as gospel truth: we must verify all methods and data, from the collection method to their transformation.

6. Public Access to Data and Accounts: All accounts and raw data of these public organizations must be made public so that their results and performance can be openly evaluated, along with the salaries of their executives, management of tenders, etc.

7. Citizen Auditors: The role of auditors must be taken by citizens, not by auditing firms intertwined with power. These administrations deliberately hide behind "data security," granting them exclusivity and resale value of data, which is an invaluable asset for nations. Every citizen should be able to access the endpoints of various public organization information systems to use de-identified data.

8. Control Over Data and Reporting Systems: Black boxes abound, and data servers and reporting systems, whether on-premises or in the cloud, which essentially replace administrative archives, must be strictly controlled, audited, and become part of the nation's intangible public heritage. This data should be used for the continuous improvement of public services and the protection of human rights, especially those of children.

9. Overcome Administrative Nightmares: These organizations intentionally create administrative nightmares to make data reconciliation and the identification of actor responsibility impossible, hiding in plain sight at the top.

By implementing these measures, we can reclaim control over the reporting and data that shape our society, ensuring transparency and accountability in public and private sectors alike.

Abandon Traditional Media for Direct Information

1. Ban Non-Citizen Media: All media outlets that are not citizen-funded and transparent should be banned. Prioritize media with transparent and citizen-based funding. Ignore all government propaganda that creates tension.

2. Break Free from Imposed Media Structures: Step out of the imposed media framework to build your own reliable information networks. This could include preaching in town squares, self-publishing books, creating videos, and more.

3. Develop a Twitter-Based Information Network: Utilize Twitter (now X), even though it is not a perfect platform. Avoid the national narrative as much as possible. Twitter is likely to become a "decentralized governance platform" in the near future. In the absence of a national actor, it is the best option currently available.

4. Create a Transparent National System to Control Mystique: At a national level, develop a transparent and effective information system. Freedom of expression must remain absolute. Intolerable comments will naturally be subjected to collective disapproval and general annoyance.

5. Understand the Role of Censorship: Censorship is unnecessary in a healthy society; it only serves to protect those in power.

Breaking Away from Hierarchical Structures and Reclaiming NGOs

1. Recognize Corruption in Hierarchies: Understand that corruption at the top of hierarchical structures leads to the decay of the entire organization. Act according to your conscience and, unless necessary, do not let yourself be driven by salary alone. Money is an illusion; it has no intrinsic value.

2. Remove Systemic Leverage: Eliminate the leverage the system has over you by any means possible. Learn about blockchain technology and digital reserve currencies, but prioritize skills, production, and bartering.

3. Rethink Retirement Systems: The French pay-as-you-go pension system, for example, is a tool of control that pushes you to act against your soul, to procrastinate, and undermines your motivation. It encourages minimal effort over a long period. Instead, we should aim to do more, not less, to ensure society functions and thrives.

4. Increase Civic Engagement: Engage in more citizen actions, create more citizen media, play more acoustic music, and increase activities in village squares. Foster more conversations and exchanges in kind.

5. Reclaim Control of NGOs: Collectively regain control over major NGOs and expel corrupt leaders. Form volunteer collectives and reclaim these organizations from the ground up. It seems that groups of five people aligned with the same ideology are sufficient to exert the necessary counter-power.

Applying Legitimate Violence and Collective Punishment

1. Reflect Collective Punishment: If collective punishment is used against you, respond in kind. Use public humiliation, discreet actions, and small pranks against those identified as corrupt.

2. Public Exposure: The first step is to make corruption public. Name, display, and photograph the corrupt individuals, as Helene Pelosse did with corrupt judges. Avoid targeting the wrong people by using an intuitive approach: if you sense something is wrong, it likely is.

3. Form Citizen Guards: In the face of armed hierarchical powers, it will be necessary to form citizen guard collectives to arrest wrongdoers and the corrupt.

4. Join Self-Defense Clubs: Joining self-defense clubs will help you integrate controlled violence and develop a local network.

Decentralization or Butlerian Jihad?

It's crucial that the programming of the new world system is decentralized to ensure essential societal poles, starting with male-female relationships, are properly balanced. Imagine if a single person held the authority to decide what defines good or evil: this is essentially the system we find ourselves in now. It eliminates all free and dissenting voices to impose a highly exacerbated Wokist ideology through the power of the state and centralized control of the media.

To counter this harmful ideology, practice legitimate violence. Similarly, any form of centralized systemic authority must be combated, and the principles of decentralization and transparency must be the foundation of the future organization.

The only alternative to the over-centralization of technology might be the Butlerian Jihad. A concept borrowed from Frank Herbert's science fiction novel *Dune*; it refers to the fight against machines that have become autonomous.

While it may seem that technology has become conscious and autonomous, be wary of the illusion; it remains in the hands of a small group.

Ancient Rites and New Cosmology

Given the profound changes in our understanding of karma and spiritual well-being, it seems that monotheistic religions and religious hierarchies have become somewhat obsolete. However, the rituals and places of worship remain vibrant, and there is a positive philosophy to be gleaned, particularly from the ideal of Christ. Kubrick and Jung both offer solutions through their work, which complement and enrich each other, as we have seen here.

Kubrick and Jung as Guides

Kubrick, born Jewish, through his filmography, and Jung, born Christian, through his alchemical writings and understanding of the human soul, provide us with a symbolic richness and depth that help us explore and establish a cosmology more suited to our time. This cosmology can be layered over the Old Testament, the Gospels, and the Quran, offering the necessary markers to avoid the turmoils humanity has experienced over the past 2500 years and helping to balance the poles.

Integrating Modern Insights with Ancient Wisdom

Wouldn't it be wonderful to see a Catholic Priest and a Muslim imam preaching Jung and Kubrick while maintaining the cultural and symbolic influence of their sacred texts? These historical narratives of origins enrich the diversity of the world. Instead of waiting for an eventual messiah, we could all become prophets in our own communities.

Focus on Universal Beauty and Life

Universal beauty transcends cultural and temporal boundaries, resonating with the innate human sense of harmony and aesthetic appreciation. In crafting a new cosmology, the pursuit and recognition of universal beauty can serve as a unifying and elevating force.

Introduction to Volume 2: The Apocalypse According to Heracles – The Subjective Experience of a Targeted Individual and the Available Technologies

In the second volume, I will narrate the barely fictionalized story of Heracles' journey to Hong Kong, individual targeted by the Western deep state in a large-scale experiment. This account will explore his confrontation with various mentioned technologies, and others yet to be revealed, leading him from Sydney to the underbelly of Hong Kong, to the Chinese border, Queen Mary Hospital, and the psychiatric wards of Pamela Youde and Castle Peak, culminating in the high-security prison of Siu Lam and his encounter with Matthew Choi, another free-spirited individual.

Bibliography

Books

[1]. Carl Gustav Jung, version texte français édition 2012 Les Arènes de Sonu Shamdasani, *Le Livre rouge*

[2]. Mike Jay, version texte anglais édition 2012 préface Oliver Sacks, *The Influencing Machine*

[3]. Fiona Barnett, version texte anglais édition spéciale Lockdown 2020, *Eyes Wide Open*

[4]. Colin A. Ross Manitou Communications 2011, *The CIA Doctors: Human Rights Violations by American Psychiatrists*

[5]. Charles T. McClenechan, 1868, *The Book of the Ancient and Accepted Scottish Rite*

[6]. Michel Ciment, Faber and Faber, 2001, *Kubrick: The Definitive Edition*

[7]. Carl Gustav Jung, *Answer to Job* et *L'homme a la découverte de son âme*

[8]. Paul Halpern, 2012, *Edge of the Universe: A voyage to the cosmic horizon and Beyond*

[9]. Frank Herbert, *Série Dune*

[10]. L'abbé Constant, 1841, *La bible de la Liberté*

[11]. Friedrich Nietzsche, 1883, *Ainsi parlait Zarathoustra*

Films

Filmographie complète de Stanley Kubrick

Roman Polanski, 1968, *Rosemary's Baby*

Roman Polanski, 1968, *Chinatown*

Richard Kelly, 2006, *Southland Tales*

Sam Esmail, 2023, *Leave the World Behind*

Articles

[12]. William J. Broad, New York Times, 01/09/2018 *Microwave Weapons Are Prime Suspect in Ills of U.S. Embassy Workers*

[13]. Stephanie Tran and Eve Cogan | Declassified Australia | 18/04/2024 *REVEALED : THE PENTAGON'S INFILTRATION OF AUSTRALIAN UNIVERSITIES*

[14]. Dimsumdaily Hong Kong, 13/10/2021 *Murder suspect Matthew Choi who killed taxi driver arrested on Lamma Island*

[15]. New York State Modern Political Archive, Carleton P. Simon Papers, 1881-1952, 1956

[16]. Daytoninmanhattan Blog, 04/2014, *The 1927 Ziegler Mansion -- No. 116 E. 55th Street*

[17]. Anderson Report - Report of the Board of Enquiry into Scientology 1965

[18]. Tim Kreider, University of California, 2000, *Introducing Sociology A Review of Eyes Wide Shut*

[19]. Eric Schlosser, New Yorker, 17/01/2014, *Almost Everything in "Dr. Strangelove" Was True*

[20]. MK Ultra Mind Control in Australia, McMurray Reports

[21]. David Salinas Flores, Faculty of Human Medicine, Universidad Nacional Mayor De San Marcos, *Mind Control: From Nazis to DARPA*

[22]. Robert C. Jones Jr., 18/03/2021, *Researcher finds a better way to tap into the brain (nanoparticules)*

[23]. *DARPA IS FUNDING NANOPARTICLES THAT PERMEATE BRAIN TO READ NEURAL SIGNALS*

[24]. Walter Pincus, The Cipher Brief, 02/01/2024 DARPA's Focus on 'Manipulated Media' Lays Out Technology for Combatting Disinformation and more

[25]. Eiichiro Komatsu (Max-Planck-Institut für Astrophysik), 3/12/ 2020, Physics of the Cosmic Microwave Background IMPRS Advanced Course & Physics of the Cosmic Microwave Background IMPRS Advanced Course

[26]. Nita Farahani, Director, Duke Initiative for Science & Society, *UN Submission 02/07/2023*

[27]. NATO, Office of the Chief Scientist NATO, *Trends 2023-2043 Across the Physical, Biological, and Information Domains*

The author, Héraclès Harixcalde

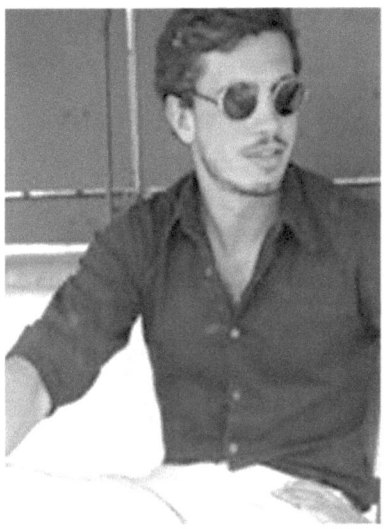

The author, a Franco-Australian analyst, specializes in strategic intelligence, big data, and artificial intelligence, particularly within the psychiatric and health services sectors. His expertise extends to identifying and addressing the disconnection between reported organizational outcomes and the actual realities on the ground, a gap that has become more pronounced since the COVID-19 pandemic.

He argues that the heart of the problem lies in the design and control of information systems and organizational structures. According to him, these are manipulated by key actors under the influence of occult and mafia-like powers, operating within a global extortion network.

In this first volume of the "Mysterium Australis" series, he makes his debut as an author, providing a critical examination of these issues through an analytical lens.

Coming soon

1. *Odysseus or A short story of Humanity,* Modern rewriting of Odysseus from Homer

2. *Mysterium Australis Volume II - Volume 2: The Apocalypse According to Heracles – The Subjective Experience of a Targeted Individual and the Available Technologies*